EFFORTLESS
Journaling

HOW TO START A JOURNAL,
MAKE IT A HABIT,
AND FIND ENDLESS WRITING

S.J. SCOTT

&

BARRIE DAVENPORT

Disclaimer

Contents

Your Free Gift

As a way of saying thanks for your purchase, we're offering a free digital product that's exclusive to readers of *Effortless Journaling*.

One of the best ways to get started is to build the "gratitude journaling" practice. So with that in mind, we are offering a free PDF version of our bestselling physical journal:

The 90-Day Gratitude Journal: A Mindful Practice for a Lifetime of Happiness.

To learn more, click (or tap) the image or link below to get free instant access.

S.J. Scott & Barrie Davenport

>> Go Here To Get Your Copy of The 90-Day Gratitude Journal <<

www.developgoodhabits.com/90day-gratitude

The Power of Journaling

Journaling can change your life.

That's a big statement, we know. But we aren't blowing smoke when we tell you that writing in a journal on a regular basis will make you healthier, happier, smarter, and more self-aware. In fact, there are so many science-backed benefits of journaling that we've devoted an entire chapter to them.

Of course, eating broccoli, standing on your head, and getting more sleep also have plenty of science-backed benefits too. So what makes journaling such a great habit?

Why make the effort to scribble in a book (or digital device) every day when you could be binging on your favorite TV show or standing on your head?

Here's the bottom line: You have this one life (as far as we know) in which you have a multitude of experiences, feelings, awakenings, ideas, longings, dreams, goals, frustrations, and worries. All of these are fleeting but critical to your evolution as a person. With a journal, you have the opportunity to capture all the thoughts in your head, tease them out, mull them over, wrestle with them, savor them, and preserve them for perpetuity.

A journal is a snapshot of you. It is an autobiography of sorts that is a continual work in progress, allowing you to process your life even as you document it. Unless you are famous or infamous, who else will treat your one valuable and amazing life with such esteem by documenting your internal and external worlds?

Your journal is your companion, your therapist, your best friend, your teacher, your punching bag, and your personal historian all rolled up in a simple book. It's inexpensive and easy to use—and it doesn't talk back. Who wouldn't want to take advantage of that?

Perhaps we've convinced you to pick up a pen and commit to journaling. But we know the hard part of the journaling habit isn't making the decision to pursue it—**it's the habit part**. It's the daily effort to carve out the time, ignore your internal excuses, and start writing. As much as we want to be committed journal writers, developing the habit can be frustrating and elusive.

How many times have you started a journal only to fizzle out after the first few entries? Or maybe you had a good go of it for a year, but now five years have passed without a single "Dear Diary." We aren't trying to shame or judge you. We (Steve and Barrie) both have stacks of unfinished journals and notebooks languishing in forgotten corners of our homes.

Steve reveals about his journaling habits in the past, "I'd get excited about writing a daily journal, and for the first week, everything would go smoothly. Then, I'd get busy one day and decide that 'missing one day won't hurt.' The next time I was busy, one missed day turned into two. Eventually, I wasn't bothering to write in my journal at all anymore."

Barrie's problem with journaling was self-judgment. She'd read her previous journal entries, think they sounded ridiculous or stupid then stop writing because she felt embarrassed about her writing abilities. Harshly judging your journal writing isn't a good strategy for continuing the habit!

Often, we pick up a journal as a reaction to something good or bad going on in our lives. We meet the love of our life, or we have a fight with our best friend and unload about these events in a journal. But until the next big event occurs, our journals sit like lonely, neglected dust-catchers on a desk or bedside table.

The key to success with a journaling habit is embracing it as a daily routine (like brushing your teeth) rather than an optional activity. Whether or not you get the promotion, argue with your spouse, feel inspired, have a case of the blues, or experience a completely uneventful day—you write.

It's the day-in, day-out consistency that makes the journaling habit so valuable. Surprisingly, those uneventful days are often the times when your journal calls you to dig deeper into your psyche to explore the untapped wellspring of feelings and ideas. You get to the marrow of your life rather than skimming the surface.

It is for that purpose that we have written this book, *Effortless Journaling: How to Start a Journal, Make It a Habit, and Find Endless Writing Topics*. Our goal is to help you get to the marrow of your life through the habit of journaling. Yes, you will enjoy many other benefits from journaling as we explore later on. But as we view it, journaling is an essential part of knowing yourself and continuing your growth as a person. It unlocks a part of you that can't be unlocked any other way.

About *Effortless Journaling*

Before we started writing this book, we surveyed our blog readers to find out the roadblocks and challenges they face when it comes to consistent journaling. Most readers want to build this habit, but have concerns holding them back.

Here are the eight most common roadblocks our readers reported:

1. *I need concrete strategies and a step-by-step process for turning journaling into a consistent habit.*

2. *Journaling feels overwhelming. I don't know what to do or how to do it.*

3. *I've tried so many times before, and I just can't stick with it.*

4. *My life is so busy that I can't find the time to journal.*

5. *My journal is never around when I need it, so I forget to write.*

6. *I have no idea what to write about. Staring at a blank page is intimidating.*

7. *I'm afraid someone will read my journal.*

8. *I don't know what kind of journal I need—there are so many types out there.*

Throughout *Effortless Journaling*, we address <u>each of these concerns</u> to help you make the journaling habit a part of your daily routine. Journaling doesn't have to be a chore. It should be enjoyable, enlightening, and something you look forward to. And it can also be a mindfulness practice that is deeply rewarding and soul-satisfying.

Specifically, we will cover the following topics to help you master the habit of journal writing:

- 15 benefits of journaling—including how it can positively

impact your physical and mental wellbeing, your productivity, and your personal life

- How to combine journaling with the practice of mindfulness
- 3 simple tools you need to get started with journaling
- 9 popular journaling strategies—and how to pick the one that's right for *you*
- 8 rules for consistent, daily journaling
- How to turn journaling into a sticky, permanent habit

You'll find that the following book is a quick read full of actionable content. And if you follow this blueprint (and apply the information), you won't feel overwhelmed, you won't give up, you will find the time to write, and you'll know exactly where your journal is when it's time to write in it.

We have a lot of ground to cover, so let's get to it!

15 Benefits of Journaling

As the number of studies increased, it became clear that writing was a far more powerful tool for healing than anyone had ever imagined.

—James W. Pennebaker

In second or third grade, most American children learn how to write in cursive. It's a thrilling time to master the art and craft of linking loopy letters into words and forming full sentences in half the time it takes to labor over print letters.

Learning handwriting is a rite of passage and allows us entrée into the broader world of ideas, analysis, and creative thought—often stimulated by the act of writing itself.

Physical therapist Suzanne Baruch Asherson says in an article[1] for *The New York Times,*

> *Learning to write in cursive is shown to improve brain development in the areas of thinking, language and working memory. Cursive handwriting stimulates brain synapses and synchronicity between the left and right hemispheres, something absent from printing and typing.*

Little did we know it in elementary school, but learning handwriting did much more for us than provide a useful means of

---

1 https://www.nytimes.com/roomfordebate/2013/04/30/
should-schools-require-children-to-learn-cursive/
the-benefits-of-cursive-go-beyond-writing

communication. It stimulated our brain and gave us a tool for self-healing and personal growth.

Most of us journal writers who grew up before computers were ubiquitous wrote by hand in our trusty diaries or journals. We scribbled about our pains and heartaches, penned bad poetry, and doodled our innermost secrets in the margins of the pages.

Of course, computers and smartphones have changed the way we do everything, including journaling. Now there are dozens of journaling apps available for typing your thoughts and feelings and tucking them behind a password, without ever using a physical journal.

Whether you are a pen-and-paper-only journal writer or you love the convenience and speed of typing, writing in any kind of journal has an array of physical, mental, and emotional benefits (backed by science) that may surprise you.

We want to share these with you as further evidence that you are making a life-affirming decision by adopting the journaling habit.

Physical and Mental Health Benefits

1. Journaling relieves stress and helps you cope with traumatic events.

Writing in a journal about your feelings associated with difficult or traumatic events will relieve your angst and improve your mental health. Writing helps you release, express, and impose structure on anxious feelings, thereby reducing stress and its impact on your health.

James W. Pennebaker, American social psychologist, author, and

Professor of Psychology at the University of Texas at Austin, wrote a groundbreaking report[2] on the association between expressive writing and mental health.

Pennebaker found that for study participants, who ranged "from children to the elderly—from honor students to maximum security prisoners," writing expressively about their feelings related to difficult events "produces long-term improvements in mood and indicators of well-being."

When participants in another writing study[3] were asked to write about traumatic events from their past, they reported less anxiety and insomnia in a follow-up 30 weeks after the study.

Additional research[4] suggests that writing benefits *all people*, not just those affected by trauma or illness. Free writing was found to be a good method for relieving stress, conflict, and anxiety for many college students (McKinney, 1976).

The Pennebaker experiment[5] also demonstrated that writing about feelings related to starting college reduced the number of illnesses requiring college freshmen to visit a health center (Pennebaker, Colder, & Sharp, 1990).

2. Journaling helps manage depression.

Journal writing is highly effective in helping people manage symptoms of depression. Although it's not a substitute for professional therapy (especially in cases of severe depression), journaling can complement other treatments in severe cases and

2 https://www.jstor.org/stable/40063169?seq=1#page_scan_tab_contents

3 http://psycnet.apa.org/record/2002-14067-002

4 http://psycnet.apa.org/record/1979-21510-001

5 http://www.scirp.org/(S(i43dyn45teexjx455qlt3d2q))/reference/ReferencesPapers.aspx?ReferenceID=1156605

can work alone as a symptom management tool for people with mild depression. Journaling can also help you track your progress as you seek treatment for depression.

A 2005 study[6] confirmed that expressive writing reduces the symptoms of depression in women recovering from domestic violence. Another study[7] revealed that participants with major depressive disorders reported significantly lower depression scores after three days of writing expressively for 20 minutes a day.

According to another study[8] by Stice, Burton, Bearman, & Rohde in 2006, journaling may also be as effective as cognitive behavioral therapy (CBT) in reducing symptoms of depression in high-risk adolescents. A different study[9] showed that college students who are vulnerable to depression can use journaling to reduce their brooding and rumination, two contributing factors of depressive symptoms.

3. Journaling helps manage anxiety.

Writing in a journal can help you address problematic thought patterns at the core of any kind of anxiety disorder. Journaling allows you to identify negative self-talk and false thinking to get to the root of your anxiety.

Journaling helps you:

- Calm your mind and clarify your thoughts
- Release pent-up emotions and stress

6 http://journals.sagepub.com/doi/abs/10.1177/1359105305049769

7 https://www.ncbi.nlm.nih.gov/pmc/articles/PMC3759583/

8 https://www.ncbi.nlm.nih.gov/pubmed/17007812

9 https://www.ncbi.nlm.nih.gov/pubmed/18410204

- Examine and release negative or unproductive thoughts
- Chronicle your experiences with anxiety
- Keep track of your challenges and your successes
- Understand the triggers that stimulate anxiety

Says Nancy S. Scherlong,[10] psychotherapist, writer, and certified journal therapist:

> *One of the primary ways in which writing helps and writing heals is by externalizing and being able to examine what was previously held internally. By being able to pace one's own experience (through pacing one's writing), greater mastery can be achieved in stressful circumstances.*

4. Journaling promotes self-reflection and self-awareness.

Although people have written diaries and journals for centuries, the therapeutic potential of reflective writing didn't come into public awareness until the 1960s, when Dr. Ira Progoff,[11] a psychologist in New York City, began offering workshops and classes in the use of what he called the intensive journal method.[12]

He developed the method to help people gain awareness about the diverse aspects of their lives, connect with their true selves, and develop more meaningful lives through the process of writing.

---

10 http://www.wellnessmetaphors.com/about/
11 https://en.wikipedia.org/wiki/Ira_Progoff
12 https://en.wikipedia.org/wiki/Intensive_journal_method

A journal provides a medium for learning more about yourself. In a study[13] about journals and reflection, researchers Spalding and Wilson revealed that self-reflection begins with doubt, hesitation, or perplexity then evolves to searching to resolve, clarify, or address doubt.

They also found that self-reflection through journaling may provide more benefit to those who are open-minded rather than people who are closed-minded. For an open-minded journal writer who is seeking awareness, a journal can be a form of self-therapy.

5. Gratitude journaling improves health and well-being.

If you want to improve your overall well-being, start a gratitude journal to document your blessings. According to a 2003 study[14] by Emmons and McCullough, gratitude journaling improves your long-term well-being, encourages exercise, reduces physical pain and symptoms, and increases both length and quality of sleep.

It increases your optimism, happiness, and health, according to Froh, Sefick, & Emmons, 2008.[15] It also makes you friendlier, more open, and more likely to engage in prosocial behaviors, enhancing and expanding your social support network (Seligman, Steen, Park, & Peterson, 2005).[16]

---

13 https://www.researchgate.net/publication/249400288_Demystifying_Reflection_A_Study_of_Pedagogical_Strategies_That_Encourage_Reflective_Journal_Writing

14 https://greatergood.berkeley.edu/images/application_uploads/Emmons-CountingBlessings.pdf

15 https://www.ncbi.nlm.nih.gov/pubmed/19083358

16 https://www.researchgate.net/publication/7701091_Positive_Psychology_Progress_Empirical_Validation_of_Interventions

6. Journaling reduces blood pressure and boosts the immune system.

According to a study[17] by Dr. James Pennebaker, journaling lowers stress and anxiety and helps manage high blood pressure. According to Pennebaker, journaling strengthens T-lymphocytes, immune cells that fluctuate with stress and anxiety. Strengthening them boosts the immune system and helps keep blood pressure low.

7. Journaling improves physical and psychological health for cardiac patients.

Researchers with The Written-Heart study[18] of coronary patients discovered that expressive writing had multiple benefits associated with many cardiovascular risk factors.

They found as little as three to five 20-minute writing sessions improved both the physical and psychological health of these patients based on health outcome measures such as number of doctor's visits and hospital days, blood pressure control, lung and immune function, pain, anxiety, and depression.

8. Journaling improves sleep.

By releasing anxious thoughts and expressing them in your journal, you prevent those thoughts and feelings from keeping you up at night—or waking you up in the middle of the night.

Writing things down helps decrease cognitive arousal, rumination,

---

17 https://utexas.influuent.utsystem.edu/en/publications/
confronting-a-traumatic-event-toward-an-understanding-of-inhibiti
18 https://www.ncbi.nlm.nih.gov/pmc/articles/PMC3151200/

and worry. When you offload these, you fall asleep faster because your problems or worries no longer agitate your mind.

A new study[19] in the *Journal of Experimental Psychology* suggests writing a to-do list for the next day in a journal for five minutes before bed helped people fall asleep an average of nine minutes faster—in about 16 minutes versus 25.

Journaling before bed can be part of a nighttime ritual that is calming and conducive to falling asleep. This is especially true if you avoid writing about something that agitates you (like your feelings about your ex or how mad you are at your neighbor).

Gratitude journaling is an excellent bedtime ritual that puts your mind at ease and reminds you of the positive parts of your life.

Productivity Benefits

9. Journaling helps you achieve your goals.

One of the best topics to journal about is what you want to achieve in the future. It's inspiring to write about your hopes and dreams, but it's more valuable to get specific by writing down quantifiable goals.

A journal is the perfect medium for brainstorming your goals, releasing your doubts and fears about them, refining them, and creating actionable steps toward reaching them. Once you write down those action steps, you can use your journal to document what you've accomplished, as well as for accountability so you are motivated to stay on track.

You'd be surprised how much more effective it is to write about your goals and your progress on them rather than just tackling

19 https://www.ncbi.nlm.nih.gov/pubmed/29058942

them without writing. A recent study[20] on writing down goals revealed that "those who wrote their goals accomplished significantly more than those who did not write their goals."

10. Journaling helps you close open loops.

Ever had a thought get stuck in your head? Perhaps you're thinking about a problem at work, or an argument with your spouse, or an all-consuming project that takes up a lot of your mental bandwidth. We all have those moments when we can't stop thinking about a particular issue. Fortunately, one of the best ways to close your open loops is to write them down in a journal, which relates to a concept commonly known as "the Zeigarnik effect."

Bluma Zeigarnik[21] first noticed something in the 1920s. She saw that waiters, with seemingly perfect recall of their dishes, couldn't remember a thing about the food after it was delivered. This led her to conduct a series of experiments where subjects were interrupted in the middle of putting together a puzzle. Those that were interrupted remembered *a lot more* about the puzzle than the subjects who were allowed to complete the task.

Furthermore, in the book *Willpower*,[22] Baumeister and Tierney discuss additional experiments in which an uncompleted task will bother you—**up until the moment when you make a plan**.

In other words, if something keeps popping into your mind, the act of writing it down and figuring out a plan for dealing with it will cause it to no longer weigh down your conscious mind.

---

20 https://www.dominican.edu/academics/lae/undergraduate-programs/psych/faculty/assets-gail-matthews/researchsummary2.pdf

21 http://en.wikipedia.org/wiki/Bluma_Zeigarnik

22 https://www.developgoodhabits.com/Willpower

Sure, journaling won't immediately "solve" the issues that you're currently dealing with. But this habit can become a critical first step to mapping out a strategy for overcoming an obstacle.

11. Journaling awakens you to opportunities.

Have you ever heard of the reticular activating system (RAS)? It's a bundle of nerves at your brainstem that filters out unnecessary information so the valuable and important stuff gets through.

Why is this relevant to journaling? Because when you journal about a goal, a question, an intention, or a need, your RAS will work overtime to ensure you pay attention to the resources and answers you're seeking. When you write down what you want, you'll be more inclined to see opportunities.

Your RAS will sift through all the data and input you receive daily to put a "blue light special" alert on the relevant information. It helps you find information that validates your beliefs or desires. This is the reason writing down your goals makes it more likely that you'll achieve them.

12. Journaling helps you overcome fears to take more action.

A journal is a great place to write down and sort through your fears and concerns about a problem or goal. As your left brain is busy writing, your right brain works on creative solutions and productive actions.

If you are writing your journal by hand, the act of handwriting itself stimulates brain synapses and synchronicity between the left and right hemispheres. Writing about your worries and problems gives you a leg up on finding the answers you seek.

In addition, once you unload your worries on paper, you no longer need to store them in your brain, giving you more mental bandwidth to brainstorm positive actions. Your journal becomes a "worry box," putting some distance between you and your problems.

Personal Benefits

13. Journaling improves your intimate relationship.

How many times have you said something to your partner or spouse in the heat of the moment, only to regret it later? What if you had written about it in your journal first, before you unleashed on your loved one?

Journaling helps you process intense emotions to address the core issue that's bothering you. Often, the things we take out on our partners have more to do with *us* than them. Whatever the case, your journal gives you the space to calm down, think about the situation, and craft a response that is more loving and thoughtful.

But a journal isn't just for relational conflict. You can use it to write down relationship goals[23] that you and your partner work on together to improve your love and intimacy. You can also journal about the positive things you notice about your spouse, focusing on gratitude for this primary person in your life.

You can use a couples' journal to ask and answer insightful questions of one another, keeping a permanent record of your relationship and how it is growing and evolving.

---

23 https://liveboldandbloom.com/02/relationships/relationship-goals

14. Journaling helps you remember and take personal inventory.

If you've kept a journal in the past, you know how enlightening it is to revisit your journal years later to get a glimpse into the mind of your former self. You're reminded of details of events, places you frequented, friendships and relationships that have changed or disappeared, and mindsets that have shifted and transformed.

Journaling is a chronicle of your life—both your interior world and the experiences and happenings of the day. Having that permanent record of your life allows you to see how you have evolved as a person. It also allows you to revisit memories, which are so often flawed, in the black-and-white transcript of your concurrent experiences, affording a more honest interpretation of life events.

15. Journaling improves your writing and communication skills.

The more you write, the better writer you become. You may not want to craft the next bestselling novel, but you likely write for work and communicate in writing with your friends and family. Being a decent writer reflects well on your character and intelligence. Writing regularly teaches you to take responsibility for your words and how you present them.

Writing in a journal also clarifies your thinking and improves your communication. When your thoughts are organized and well-articulated on paper, you will express ideas and experiences better verbally. All of that personal written communication in your journal improves your vocabulary, helps you store ideas in your memory, and makes articulating those ideas much easier.

Depending on the *type of journal* you choose to write, you can enjoy dozens of additional benefits—boosting your confidence, enhancing your reading skills, planning out difficult conversations, documenting travel or a special interest, tracking your meditation practice, remembering your dreams, and so many more.

There is no question that journaling has tremendous therapeutic and practical value in your life. If you work on no other habit this year, you'll find that journaling alone will foster so many positive changes that you'll wonder why you haven't nurtured the habit every day of your life.

Now, there is one last benefit of journaling—it can be powerfully combined with a concept commonly known as "mindfulness." So let's talk about that next.

How to Combine Journaling with Mindfulness

Ten times a day something happens to me like this—some strengthening throb of amazement—some good sweet empathic ping and swell. This is the first, the wildest and the wisest thing I know: that the soul exists and is built entirely out of attentiveness.

—Mary Oliver

One of the best aspects of journaling is how it can be incorporated into an existing mindfulness habit, especially when you use it for more than chronicling the day's events.

Mindfulness is the practice of being fully present and engaged in whatever you are doing in the moment. When you are mindful, you are intentionally aware of the present moment. You consciously direct your awareness to whatever you are doing, thinking, or observing.

With the habit of journaling, your mind is fully engaged in your writing. Writing (especially by hand) forces your brain to slow down to better organize your thoughts and consider the big picture or a different perspective.

In the flow of journaling, past regrets and future worries lose their edge. You, your mind, and your pen and paper merge in the present moment. This state of mindful flow occurs regardless of the topic you are journaling about, as long as you are engaged in the process and find it enjoyable or cathartic.

The act of writing keeps us tethered to the present moment, so we can take a step back from our worries and preoccupations. Thus, we become more acutely aware of ourselves as the witness or agent of our experiences, thoughts, and feelings, removing us a step further from the intensity of our feelings and giving us *the choice* for nonjudgmental observation and necessary action.

When you are journaling mindfully, you engage in a creative process that requires no final product that must be evaluated. Journaling remains a process—never an outcome. Says Jon Kabat-Zinn, bestselling author and creator of the Stress Reduction Clinic and the Center for Mindfulness in Medicine, Health Care, and Society,[24] "Mindfulness means paying attention in a particular way; on purpose, in the present moment, and nonjudgmentally."

Mindfulness also strengthens the creative flow of writing, and writing can strengthen mindfulness. Getting into the habit of writing down your feelings, thoughts, and observations in a journal helps you hone your skills of noticing. It also gives you space for the unfolding of whatever arises in your mind as you prepare to write with pen hovering over paper.

When was the last time you really paid attention to the wind fluttering the leaves on the trees or the sounds of nature as you stepped outside to start your day? As you begin your journaling habit, you'll discover you feel more present in daily life and pay more attention to the unnoticed subtleties of the world around you.

This new awareness gives you pages and pages of things to write about. You will be flooded with thoughts, feelings, memories, and observations that beg to be released and explored on paper.

---

24 https://www.umassmed.edu/cfm/

But journaling expands mindfulness beyond just paying attention because you learn to pay attention *with intention and purpose* as Jon Kabat-Zinn suggests. When you willingly and actively come to your journal to write, you pause and carve out the time to explore your feelings and observations in a deeper and more compelling way.

A journal practice also allows you to start a dialogue within yourself about your inner and outer worlds. It affords clarity where there was none, which is an innate gift of mindfulness. When you pay attention, life becomes pristinely clear.

The mindfulness connection to journaling gives you yet another powerful reason to adopt the journal-writing habit. In fact, we invite you to approach journaling as a mindfulness activity. Approach it with a sense of reverence and joyful anticipation. Rather than viewing it only as a good-for-you habit you should adopt, embrace it as a ritual that gives meaning to your life.

Here are four ideas for developing your journaling practice as a mindfulness activity:

1. Create a peaceful journaling space.

If you journal from your home most of the time, create a peaceful writing space that inspires you and makes you feel good. This is part of making the habit a ritual that includes actions and items that imbue the activity with meaning and importance.

Maybe you sit at a special desk you love. You might want to write in front of a window with a beautiful view. Perhaps you like being surrounded by books. You might prefer a minimalist room with few visual distractions. Consider lighting a candle, using the soft light of a lamp, or putting on relaxing music.

Do whatever you can to make your journaling space conducive to mindfulness and creativity. Visit Pinterest and type "writing spaces"[25] in the search bar for some creative ideas for your journaling nook.

2. Minimize distractions.

You can't stay focused and attentive to your journal writing efforts if your phone is buzzing, your cat keeps hopping in your lap, and emails are dinging on your computer. Put your phone out of sight and turn it off. Lock the cat out of your room. Ask your family not to bother you. Clear your desk of anything that might draw your attention away.

If you are writing in a notebook or physical journal, all you need is your page and your pen. If you are writing on a computer or journaling app, shut down any other browsers or notifications that could distract you.

Mindful journaling requires interruption-free and distraction-free time, so you will need to prepare and plan for this in advance.

3. Begin with a short meditation.

The best way to calm and clear your mind before you begin writing is with a short centering meditation. Just a few minutes is enough to feel more calm and focused, especially if your journaling time follows a particularly busy or hectic part of your day.

Here are the simple steps for this meditation:

---

25 https://www.pinterest.com/search/pins/?q=writing spaces&rs=typed&term_meta%5b%5d=writing%7Ctyped&term_meta%5b%5d=spaces%7Ctyped

- Sit on a cushion on the floor or in a chair. Don't get too comfortable—you don't want to fall asleep!

- Let your hands fall gently into your lap. Close your eyes, and take a few deep and cleansing breaths until you feel calm.

- Notice any tension or discomfort in your body, and focus your breathing into those places, inviting them to relax.

- Continue breathing normally, focusing on each breath and noticing the air entering your lungs and exiting as you exhale.

- After a few minutes of focused breathing, as you inhale, imagine all of your scattered energies rushing back from out in the world, into the center point of your body.

View these energies as white, peaceful, healing rays that you are breathing in. Envision them filling your center with calm and contentment.

As you exhale, envision all of the stress, confusion, anxiety, and busyness leaving your body and floating away out of sight.

Continue with this breathing and visualization until you feel calmly energized and centered in yourself again.

This meditation should take only five to ten minutes, but if you don't have much time, simply close your eyes and focus your breathing for a few minutes to feel less agitated and more mentally available for journaling.

4. Stay aware, and take notice.

Your journal is a beautiful tool for exploring and examining your life and the world around you. But if you aren't paying attention, you're depriving yourself of the richness and beauty available to inspire your writing.

We get so absorbed in our daily activities and demands that we fail to lift our heads and notice what's around us. We're so focused on pain from the past or worries for the future that there's little mental space to experience and savor the present moment.

A journal is a great way to process and relieve the stress of daily demands and life worries, but there is so much more a journal can do for you when you're attentive to the world around you and your own feelings and thoughts.

You may want to jot down reminders or quick notes (in your phone or a small notepad) during the day to prompt you for journaling in the evening or the next morning. Life is a marvelous idea bucket for journaling, so tune into it and use it as a resource.

To increase your mindfulness as well as your feelings of happiness, use the world around you as inspiration to journal about experiences or situations that lead to feelings of:

- well-being, gratitude, or fulfillment;
- a sense of purpose, significance, or alignment with your values;
- being in the flow where time stands still;
- enthusiasm and joy;
- admiration or deep interest in someone or something.

These experiences or situations can arise during your workday, in interactions with loved ones, or during your non-working hours when you are engaged in a hobby or task. You can also explore these feelings when watching a movie or TV show, reading something in a book or on the Internet, or simply being outside in nature.

The key is to pay attention. Be aware of what you are doing and how it makes you feel.

Later in the book, we discuss mindfulness journaling in more depth and provide instructions on using a journal to chronicle and explore other mindfulness practices. But we want to reinforce the mindfulness aspect of all journaling styles here at the beginning of the book so you can approach this valuable habit with a sense of presence and enthusiasm.

All right, now that you understand the main benefits of journaling, let's take that first step to building the habit. We'll start with the three basic tools you will need to set out on the right foot (or hand!).

3 Journaling Tools to Get Started

Do not wait; the time will never be "just right." Start where you stand, and work with whatever tools you may have at your command, and better tools will be found as you go along.

—George Herbert

Journaling is one of the least expensive and most uncomplicated practices you can adopt. You don't need many tools, and the ones you do need don't have to be fancy or costly. Don't let the idea that you must have a leather-bound journal or a gold-plated fountain pen hold you back from getting started. A good old BIC pen and a $0.99 spiral notebook will get the job done just as well.

In fact, there are only three tools you need to begin journaling:

1. A Notebook (or Digital Device)

There are two options for journaling: a physical journal or a digital journal. Both are fine, but we lean toward the physical journal option.

Physical Journal

As we mentioned earlier, there are many benefits to journaling the old-fashioned way—in longhand. Handwriting sharpens critical thinking, allows for better short- and long-term memory recall, and helps you develop a stronger conceptual understanding than typing does. Because handwriting is slower and more tedious, you are forced to process thoughts and information, as your brain must mentally engage with what you are writing.

Also, handwriting allows you additional creativity with journaling. You may like to doodle, highlight, mind map, and use various colors as part of your journaling. Some of this can be done on a computer, but it doesn't reflect your personal style as much as doing it by hand.

For these reasons, we recommend handwriting your journal, and there are several inexpensive options to choose from (for the sake of simplicity, we've listed each of these items in U.S. prices, but XE offers a great online conversion tool you can use to convert the amounts into your local currency[26]):

- **A spiral notebook or one-dollar journal** you can purchase from a local Dollar Store or Dollar Tree. An inexpensive notebook is a great option if you're just getting started with journaling and don't know if you'll like it. But we also know people who have stacks of spiral notebook journals they've kept over the years, and they never stray from them.

- **A Moleskine notebook** with a soft or hard cover, which runs about $9.00 to $15.00 on Amazon, depending on the size and style you choose.

- **A decorative, hard or soft bound journal** for those who want a journal cover that's more eye-catching, inspiring, or reflective of their personality. These can run the gamut in price from a few dollars to $15.00 or more.

- **A leather-bound journal** if you want an elegant, timeless look for your journal. These tend to be more expensive and

---

26 https://www.xe.com/currencyconverter/

can cost upward of $40 or more. If you go this route, be sure to choose a journal that has refillable pages.

- **A bullet journal** for jotting down thoughts, ideas, and lists (if you prefer not to write paragraphs of information in your journal). We'll talk more about bullet journals later, but for now it's good to know you can use this strategy in conjunction with a basic notebook or purchase the official Bullet Journal or a similar product on Amazon for as little as $7.00.

- **A journal with prompts** that focus on a specific topic (mindfulness, gratitude, questions, etc.) and adds structure to the journaling process. These are generally more expensive (because they require the time of a writer and designer) and can range from $10.00 to over $20.00 on Amazon, depending on the journal you select. We will discuss journals with prompts in more detail in the next chapter.

With so many options available, it can be confusing to know what kind of journal to choose. Consider the following factors as you determine the type of journal that best suits your needs.

1. Size of Journal

The size of the journal you choose depends on how you want to use it. Will you use the journal only at home, or do you want something small that you can carry with you? Does it need to be slim to fit into a computer case or coat pocket? Or do you prefer a larger journal with a lot of room to write, draw, and make notes?

Some standard sizes include, from smallest to largest:

- Micro: 70 x 90 mm | 2.75" x 3.625"
- Mini: 95 x 140 mm | 4" x 5.5"
- Midi: 120 x 170 mm | 5" x 7"

- Slim: 90 x 180 mm | 3.75" x 7"
- Ultra: 180 x 230 mm | 7" x 9"
- Grande: 210 x 300 mm | 8.25" x 11.75"

2. Binding and Cover

Do you prefer a journal that will lay flat on a surface? If so, you might consider a coil- or spiral-bound journal, although lefties often complain their writing hand rubs against the coil.

Some book-bound journals will lay flat if they are larger and if you break the spine. You want to be sure the book is bound well so pages don't come loose and fall out.

Some journal writers prefer a hardback cover to a paperback because it's sturdier and more durable and has a more distinguished look. But it can be harder to get a hardbound journal to remain open without holding it open with one hand.

Staple binding is also an option most often used with pocket-size notebooks or journals that don't have many pages.

3. Cover Design

Are you fine with a plain cover for your journal, or do you want something that reflects your personal style? The right cover design can inspire the writer. But, then again, once the journal is open for writing, you won't see the cover.

If you are taking your journal to the local coffee shop or on business travel, you may want a cover that is innocuous and without a design or title that might make you (or others) uncomfortable.

4. Paper Quality

Any kind of paper might work just fine for you, or you may prefer something higher-grade that has a smooth finish, with a high opacity so you don't see your writing on the reverse side of the page, and very little feathering (when the ink spreads out on the page).

Paper quality is a personal preference, but if you intend to keep your journals for a long time, you might want to consider a higher quality paper.

However, the type of pen you choose will impact your decision on paper choice. Paper that's too thin can leave indentions on the remaining blank pages. However, if you choose a fountain pen, it will feather on thicker, higher quality paper.

If you're particular about your paper and pen, you might go to a paper or stationery store and test writing with various pens on different types of paper.

5. Page Count

Do you want a yearly journal with 365 separate pages to write every day or a smaller journal with fewer pages that works for a month or two? In general, the fewer pages, the smaller and lighter the journal.

But fewer pages means you have to continue buying journals or notebooks. There are some journals made to write in for several years, but you'll find there isn't a lot of room to write for each daily entry.

6. Blank, Ruled, or Gridded

Are you enticed by a large swath of white paper begging for you to fill it? If so, you might enjoy a journal with completely blank, unlined pages. This is a good choice for someone who might want to draw or doodle in their journal or someone who prefers a more free-form style of journaling.

People who prefer to stay within the lines usually like a ruled journal. If this is your choice, pay attention to how much space there is between the lines. If your writing is big and loopy, you may need more space. If you have an accountant's handwriting, then you'll do fine with narrower lines. College ruled is the standard, at 7 mm.

Gridded graph paper, which comes in 5 mm, is also good for tiny handwriting, mind-mapping, and creating lists.

7. Closure

You may or may not want a journal with a closure. If you do, there are a few options. You can get a traditional diary with a lock and key if you're worried about privacy. You can find journals with metal clasps, elastic bands, ties, or magnetic clasps.

Consider a closure if you will be inserting papers, photos, or other loose items into your journal and don't want them to fall out. A closure (that isn't a lock and key) won't prevent others from reading your journal, but it might discourage someone from taking a peek.

8. How You'll *Use* the Journal

The way you want to use your journal is the most important factor in deciding the type of journal to purchase. If you are writing down daily musings without any particular structure, any basic notebook or bound journal will work just fine.

- If you're using the journal to write lists or work on a particular goal, you may want to consider a bullet journal— although a notebook would work just fine for that as well.

- If you're writing a journal as a long-term keepsake or something to pass on to your family, you might want a sturdier, more decorative journal.

- If you want direction for your journal writing on a specific topic or interest, consider a journal with prompts that ask questions or tell you what to write about.

We will discuss various types of journaling throughout the book, so if you aren't sure what kind of journaling (and journal) is best for you, you'll have a much better idea once you finish reading.

Digital Journal

You can bypass much of this journal decision-making by opting to do your journal-writing on your computer or smartphone. Although there are benefits to handwriting your journal entries, there are plenty of good reasons why you might choose to journal with a device. Here are few of the benefits of digital journaling:

- It can be more convenient, as we tend to carry a digital device everywhere we go.

- Typing (rather than writing longhand) is quicker, easier, and (for some) less stressful on hands and fingers.

- It's easier to edit content and check spelling.

- Many digital journals can be accessed on multiple platforms like a Mac, iPhone, and iPad.

- It's easier to keep your journal entries private with a passcode on your device.

- If you want to share your journal entries, you can easily do that on social media or email with a digital journal.

- A digital journal can date and time stamp your entries and record other info like your location and the weather.

- It's simpler to archive and review many years' worth of journals with a digital device. You don't have to store your journals as you would with a physical journal.

- You can back up a digital journal on an external hard drive without worrying about your journals being destroyed by water damage or fire.

- A digital journal can include photos, icons, graphs, and other graphics to enhance your writing.

- If you can't type or write for some reason (or you just don't feel like it), you can use voice-to-text dictation with a digital journal.

- According to a 2014 digital journaling study, "The 30-Day Digital Journaling Challenge,"[27] digital journaling provides the same benefits as writing by hand, with no sacrifice of emotional expression.

- The same study suggests that men tend to prefer writing by keyboard rather than writing by hand.

If you think a digital journal is the way to go for you, there are a variety of options to choose from. Let's review some of them to help you make the best decision.

---

27 http://www.write4life.us/wp-content/uploads/2015/12/The-30-Day-Digital-Journaling-Challenge-092615.pdf

1. A Word or Pages document is a pretty straightforward way to keep a digital journal. You type in it just as you would write with a physical journal, dating your entries and typing them out. You can save the document in a password-protected folder on your computer. If you don't need a lot of bells and whistles and just want to write, this is a simple option.

2. The Day One App[28] is a free journaling app for iPhone, iPad, Mac, and Android users (premium features are $3.99 per month). It has a secure sync function that allows you to easily switch between these devices.

It includes end-to-end encryption so your data remains private but also allows you to share entries by email, social media, or on a web page. Day One includes a variety of elegant features for a great writing experience as well as inspirational quotes and reminders to motivate you.

No matter your journaling goals (lifelogging, self-improvement, mental health, work goals, etc.), Day One is an excellent option.

3. The JRNL app[29] is another free journaling app that offers the same features as Day One, but you don't have to pay a monthly fee for premium features. It allows you to curate your entries by topic, asks hundreds of questions about your life to stimulate your writing efforts, and includes the ability to customize your journal with wallpapers and media.

You can publish a full-color, hardbound book from your journal entries of up to 900 pages for an additional fee. JRNL app is not available for Android users.

---

28 http://dayoneapp.com/
29 https://jrnl.com/

4. The Journey app[30] is an elegantly designed app with lots of white space, five beautiful fonts to choose from, an easy-to-use UI, and a completely customizable format. It works for Mac, Windows, iOS, Android, Chrome OS, and the Web. It offers tiered pricing with free, premium, and cloud options.

The premium package is a one-time purchase with additional features, and it costs about $5.00 on mobile and $9.00 on desktop. The Cloud membership option is a subscription that can be paid monthly or annually and applies across all channels. It offers you inspirational daily quotes, geo-tags your entries, and automatically records the weather.

5. The GoodNotes app[31] is compatible with iPhone, iPad, and iPod touch (it requires iOS 8.0 or later) and costs $7.99. It's a great option if you prefer bullet journaling, mind-mapping, or writing shorter journal entries.

It also has the benefits of both a digital and a handwritten journal, as it allows you to do the exact same things you can do with a paper bullet journal. You write on your device with an Apple stylus pencil, sketch diagrams, and organize your journal entries on a beautiful bookshelf.

A file in the GoodNotes app is just like an actual notebook and has separate pages you can flip through horizontally. You can also copy and reorder pages and can even convert handwriting to text.

It comes with a configurable template library to suit your journaling needs. All images or single-page PDFs are supported. You can drag and drop documents, notes, images, texts, and more in and out of GoodNotes.

---

30 https://journey.cloud/
31 https://www.goodnotes.com/

Evernote

Evernote[32] is a cross-platform tool that allows you to take notes, capture ideas, and organize this information into a file structure that's based on your personal needs. You can use Evernote to create simple text-based notes, upload photos, record voice reminders, add videos, and clip specific web pages. Anything that can be digitized can be uploaded to Evernote.

Steve uses Evernote as a central location to capture any important idea or thought. It's a great tool for noting a strategy you'd like to implement, a website you want to bookmark, or a time marker needed to record a multimedia file. Basically, whenever you come across a piece of information that's important for your long-term success, it should go into Evernote.

When it comes to journaling, Steve keeps a notebook with all of his yearly goals. Then once a week he reviews each goal, jots down his "wins" for the last seven days, describes any obstacles he encountered, and makes a plan for the next week. In essence, this Evernote file acts as an ongoing diary for the important things in his life.

This is *just one example* of how Evernote can be used in conjunction with building a journaling habit. We suggest you check out Evernote to see how it can be incorporated into your life.

There are dozens of other journaling apps available for free or for a fee. If none of the apps we've outlined here fits the bill for you, we suggest you do an online search for "best journaling apps" and do additional research. Once you finish this book and determine the type of journaling you want focus on, you may have a better idea of the app that suits your needs.

---

32 https://evernote.com/

A Blog

Finally, creating a blog is an alternative to digital journaling if you want to improve a particular area of your life and share your thoughts in a public way. This public platform helps you stay accountable to writing and has the benefit of creating interaction and connection with other like-minded people.

Steve and Barrie both have blogs related to their personal interests (*Develop Good Habits*[33] and Live Bold and Bloom,[34] a self-improvement blog, respectively). Their blogs serve not only as personal outlets but are also platforms for their online businesses.

Other bloggers use their sites as mediums for documenting a life experiment or personal journey, such as Chris Bailey's A Year of Productivity[35] (now *A Life of Productivity*), Cait Flanders's The Year of Less,[36] and Joshua Becker's Becoming Minimalist.[37]

2. A Pen or Pencil

If you choose to write in a physical journal, you'll need a pen or a pencil. If you like to sketch or doodle in your journal, a pencil or a set of colored pencils might work well for you. Also, if you want to make changes in your journal, a pencil with an eraser gives you that option without leaving those ugly scribbles and strikethroughs.

You can choose a good old #2 that you sharpen (some journal

---

33 https://www.developgoodhabits.com/
34 https://liveboldandbloom.com/
35 https://alifeofproductivity.com/
36 https://caitflanders.com/
37 https://www.becomingminimalist.com/

writers swear by Blackwings[38]) or go for a mechanical pencil if you like the feel of it and prefer to replace the lead. However, the graphite in pencils is powder and will slowly fade away over time, so a pencil isn't a good option if you want to preserve your journals for your grandchildren.

Most journal writers choose a pen because it's more permanent, elegant, and fluid. You can still doodle with a pen, and you can find pens in a variety of colors if you want to jazz up your journal.

You don't have to spend a lot of money on a pen—a pack of BIC pens will set you back about a dollar. There are hundreds of options for pens; choosing one ultimately comes down to your personal preference and the type of journaling you plan to do. Here are some pens to consider:

Ballpoint Pens

Ballpoint pens are the most affordable and practical pens you can buy (and find at any local store). The ink in a ballpoint pen has a very thick paste that creates somewhat of a drag when you write because you have to force the ball to roll to produce the ink. The ink is quick-drying, doesn't smear, and won't bleed through your paper.

These pens have the longest write-out of any pen—about 1.2 miles on average—and they have the longest shelf life. However, they aren't as smooth as gel or roller pens, and the ink doesn't absorb into the paper but, rather, sits on top of it. For archival writing, they aren't the best choice.

---

38 https://blackwing602.com/

Roller Ball Pen

Roller ball pens[39] have ink that is very fluid, and they produce a finer line than ballpoint pens. They are always capped because they can wick out when coming into contact with paper. The roller ball requires very little movement or friction for the ink to be released from the tip, making for a smooth writing experience.

Roller ball pens are fade proof, waterproof, difficult to smear, and come in a wide variety of colors. Although they aren't as cheap as a ballpoint pen, roller ball pens are still quite affordable. However, they don't last as long as a ballpoint pen, they can leak if not capped, and they stain fabrics.

Archival Pens

Archival ink is designed to be resistant to weathering and fading so that it will last for a long time. The chemically stable, pigment-based ink will not bleed or run if liquids are spilled on it.

There are many brands of archival pens available at various prices. You can get a five-pack of EK Tools journaling pens[40] on Amazon for under $9.00 or a set of Sakura Pigma Micron pens[41] for under $13.00. Micron pens have a felt tip so there is less smudge risk compared to a ballpoint. If you want some variety in your journaling, you can find sets of colored micron pens as well that come in a variety of point sizes.

If you want your journal writing to last for years, archival pens are

39 https://www.amazon.com/uni-ball-Vision-Rollerball-Point-0-7mm/dp/B00006IE8J

40 https://www.amazon.com/EK-Tools-55-30077-5-Pack-Journaling/dp/B00DN65V1Q

41 https://www.amazon.com/Sakura-Pigma-Micron-0-25-mm-Point/dp/B007SQ71F6

the way to go. You might also choose an artist-grade sketchbook for your journal, which has archival paper.

Sharpie Fine Point Pen

A Sharpie fine point pen[42] is a go-to favorite for many journal writers because it is affordable, durable, and very well made. It was the first pen-style permanent marker. The fine point creates smooth, sharp lines and allows you to write clearly and legibly in smaller spaces.

If you like to write in calligraphy style, this pen will work well for you. It dries quickly and won't smudge, but it can bleed through depending on the paper you choose.

The Sharpie fine point pen is available in a wide variety of colors that you can purchase in a pack for about $14.00.

Gel Pen

A gel pen is an excellent, inexpensive option for journal writers who want to add a little pizzazz to their journaling efforts, while maintaining a smooth and controlled look. Gel pens[43] use a water-based gel, making the ink thick and opaque. It has the permanence of oil-based ballpoint ink but glides smoothly like water-based ink.

Gel pens can produce rich and bold lines, and because the ink flows so easily, they are more comfortable to use since you don't have to press the pen too firmly onto the page. The ink in a gel pen dries fairly quickly, but left-handers (like Steve) don't

---

42 https://www.amazon.com/Sharpie-1802225-Assorted-Colors-6-Count/dp/B005LU2QA6

43 https://www.amazon.com/Paper-Mate-Retractable-Assorted-1951636/dp/B019QBOG3U

generally like gel pens because they can smear when the writer's hand drags across the page. The other downside is if you leave the cap off of a gel pen, the ink dries up in a short amount of time.

Gel pens can differ in style, shape, print, and grips, and they come in a wide range of colors and pigments (fluorescent, pastel, metallic, glitter, etc.). The ink shows up easily on dark or smooth surfaces. Gel pens do use more ink than other pens, requiring more frequent refills.

Fountain Pen

If you love the romantic beauty of ink on paper and want something elegant for your journal writing, you should consider a fountain pen.[44] Fountain pens are smooth and offer low pressure and low-angle writing.

Says Dr. Donald S. Whitney, author of *Simplify Your Spiritual Life*, in a guest post[45] on *Edgar's Emporium*:

> *I enjoy writing in my journal with a fountain pen. Yes, an old-fashioned fountain pen. And whether a new model or a "vintage" pen, with a stiff nib or a flexible one, a good fountain pen is a pleasure to write with. Even the ritual of pausing to draw ink from a bottle into a thirsty pen can bring a sense of nostalgic satisfaction in our high-tech, efficiency-driven world.*

Some writers won't use anything but a fountain pen, and you will find hundreds of styles and looks to choose from. If you prefer a fountain pen, be sure to pair it with a journal that's created with fountain pen–friendly paper to avoid bleed-through.

---

44 https://www.amazon.com/Pilot-Metropolitan-Collection-Fountain-91111/dp/B00KRPFD96

45 http://www.edgarsemporium.com/blog/2016/2/12/journal-with-a-fountain-pen

Fountain pens can be expensive and more of a hassle than you want to deal with. You have to fill the pen regularly, it takes time for the ink to dry on your paper, and the ink can smudge. You need to be careful that the ink from one page of writing doesn't transfer to the next page.

Before you choose your pen, we encourage you to decide on the type of journal you want to write in. If you choose a basic spiral notebook, then a fountain pen wouldn't be a great option. You want to match your writing tool to the paper quality and the type of writing you'll be doing. Also, think about how important it is that the ink has longevity and how much drawing or doodling you might be doing in your journal.

Once you decide on a journal, go to a stationery or art supply store and test a few pens on one of the blank pages in the back of the journal or on another page you don't mind marking up. Pay attention to:

- How the pen feels in your hand—both grip and weight
- The ease with which it moves across the paper
- Whether it bleeds through
- Whether the ink dries quickly or smears
- How it looks on the page
- If it comes in the color(s) you want
- If it's affordable for you

3. A Habit Tracking Tool

Journaling is like any other habit—you need a daily reminder to do it, otherwise it'll be easy to forget. That's why we highly recommend that you use a reminder system to prompt you into action. You can use the classic method of putting this habit on a calendar or use Post-it Notes. You can even put alerts on your phone to remind you when to journal. But since we all now live in an increasingly digital age, we recommend using an app to track the journaling habit (and all other habits you'd like to build). We like these four apps in particular:

- StridesApp.com[46]
- Coach.me[47]
- HabitHub[48]
- Todoist[49]

Out of this list, Steve recommends Todoist as the best option because not only can you use it to track your habits, you can create and manage all the projects you have in your personal and professional life. Todoist isn't difficult to use. All you have to do is create a habit and set it up as a daily, recurring action item. If you'd like to learn more about this habit, Steve has a free step-by-step tutorial on his website.[50]

Now that you've reviewed the three tools you need to begin your journaling habit, it's time to determine the best type of journal for you. In the next section, we will detail nine types of journals and journaling techniques for you to consider.

---

46 https://www.stridesapp.com/
47 https://www.coach.me/
48 http://www.thehabithub.com/
49 http://todoist.com
50 http://developgoodhabits.com/todoist-tutorial/

9 Popular Journaling Strategies

There are a thousand thoughts lying within a man that he does not know till he takes up the pen to write.

—William Makepeace Thackeray

A pen.

A blank piece of paper.

A willing mind.

How many times have we poised our pens over this paper, ready to pour out our hearts, only to falter because we have no idea what to write?

What should I say? Who might read it? How will it sound? Why am I even doing this?

Writer's block doesn't just happen to authors. It can happen to anyone who is given the chance to write about anything. The choices are too endless—it freezes the brain. Some amount of structure is required to avoid the journaling brain freeze, and that structure begins with knowing *your reason* for journaling in the first place.

- What do you want to accomplish with journaling?
- Are you hoping to process difficult emotions?
- Do you want to work on being more mindful?
- Are you thinking of focusing on gratitude?

- Are you considering a goal you want to journal about?

- Do you want to catalog your daily activities?

- Do you want to just write a stream of consciousness?

There are as many options for journaling as there are ideas in your head. It's up to you to decide where you want the journaling journey to take you. And if you make journaling a lifetime habit, you'll have the opportunity to try many different types of journaling projects. That is the beauty of this habit—it has endless possibilities and benefits.

To help you get started with your *next* journaling project, we will review nine types of journaling techniques to stimulate ideas. For each one, we cover:

- Description and basic information about the journaling technique

- The advantages and disadvantages of the journaling technique

- Who this technique is best suited for

- How to get started

- Resources that will teach you more about this type of journaling

We encourage you to read through all of these ideas before you settle on one. You might find that your initial journaling plan takes a new direction as you discover different ways to apply this habit. Are you ready to get started? Let's dive in.

4: Daily Diary

I kept a diary right after I was born. Day 1: Tired from the move. Day 2: Everyone thinks I'm an idiot.
    —Steven Wright

When we think of a diary writer, we often envision an adolescent girl unleashing her angst with a sparkly pen in a locked diary, using way too many exclamation points and dotting her i's with hearts. It's true, preteens and teenagers are avid diary writers. Research[51] shows a whopping 83% of girls aged 16 to 19 archive their lives in a private diary.

But teen girls aren't the only people who have turned to an old-fashioned diary as a place to record their daily ideas and life events. Diaries have been around for centuries, and some famous women and men depended on their diaries to record the important events of their lives and their feelings about them. Lewis Carroll, Samuel Pepys, Virginia Woolf, Anne Frank, and Harry Truman all kept diaries that were later published.

So what's the difference between a diary and a journal?

The word "diary" comes from the Latin *diarium*, meaning "daily allowance." When you write in your diary, you are recording your daily allowance of ideas and opinions, organized by date.

A diary tends to be more personal, with the focus on writing daily about personal events and the writer's thoughts and reactions to these experiences. It is a place to write notes and quotes and to record important milestones in your life that have some sort of significance—like birthdays, anniversaries, births, and deaths.

---

51 https://www.drg.global/our-work/case-studies/
channel-4-personal-diary-v-social-media-research/

Journal writing expands the idea of writing in a diary, allowing more freedom in the frequency of writing, the topics you write about, and the amount you write.

Advantages of Keeping a Daily Diary

- Diaries are great for documenting important daily and life events and keeping them organized by date.

- Diaries are good for privacy, as diaries often come with a lock.

- Diaries are generally small in dimension and bound for sturdiness and longevity.

Disadvantages of Keeping a Daily Diary

- Diaries may seem too old-fashioned or too youthful in design.

- Diaries may be too restrictive based on the type of writing you wish to do.

- Diaries may be too small if you prefer to write a lot or have large handwriting.

Who Is It For?

A diary might work best for ...

- Anyone who prefers an open structure and doesn't want to be confined by prompts, guidelines, or a set structure.

- Any who likes to keep a daily record of their thoughts, feelings, activities, and life milestones.

- Anyone who wants to keep their writing private in a locked book.

How to Get Started with a Daily Diary

1. Select the type of diary you want to use.

When you choose a diary, find one that feels good to you and compels you to write in addition to meeting the practical needs you may have for it. Some diaries are more like planners, providing just a small amount of space for writing down events and goals for the day. These often have a space to schedule each hour of the day. A traditional diary will have some sort of closure (a lock, tie, or band) and will have space for the date and blank lines for daily writing. You can find diaries with hardback, paper, leather, or plastic covers. Prices range from around $10.00 to over $20.00 for adult diaries on Amazon, but if you don't want to spend a lot of money, you can use a small notebook and replicate the interior layout of diaries you like.

2. Keep your diary with you every day.

You might want to choose a diary small enough to comfortably keep in your purse or briefcase so you have it with you whenever inspiration strikes. This will help ensure you maintain the writing habit. Or if you decide to write in your diary after a specific trigger, put your diary in a spot where it's readily available after your trigger habit.

3. Date your daily entries in your diary.

That's the point of a diary, after all—to have your daily thoughts and events chronicled so you can look back on them in the future. This daily practice will reinforce a long-term habit of writing in your diary.

4. Record something daily.

Use your diary to write down your daily goals, your thoughts and ideas, what you do each day, major (or minor) life events, and interactions you have with others. You can even write down your dreams in your diary. Some diarists enjoy collecting photos and keepsakes in their diaries.

5. Don't edit, censor, or judge your writing.

Express yourself as you wish without critiquing your entries. This isn't a school project or a writing competition. You are writing for yourself and your own enjoyment. Grammatical errors, spelling mistakes, or faulty syntax aren't important except to the extent that you can understand what you've written.

Resources

- AmazonBasics Classics Notebook:[52] An inexpensive notebook offers a no-frills approach to journaling.
- Daily Diary:[53] A digital tool that can be used to maintain your diary.

---

52 https://www.amazon.com/AmazonBasics-NH130210120V-R-Classic-Notebook-Ruled/dp/B01DN8TCEU/

53 https://www.dailydiary.com/

2: Prompt Journaling

I write in a journal daily. This extraordinary ritual has revolutionized my mindset, transformed my heartset, and generally influenced my life exponentially.

—Robin S. Sharma

As we've discussed, one of the challenges with traditional journaling is getting stuck wondering what to write about. Your brain locks up, and you just can't think of anything compelling or interesting to put in your journal.

Or maybe you have a boring day when the only thing you can report are the TV shows you watched or the number of laundry loads you completed. It almost doesn't seem worth the effort to write in your journal at a time like that.

This lack of clarity is one of the reasons people don't stick with journaling—whenever they're distracted and can't think of what to write, they skip a day. One skipped day turns into another, and the person drops the habit. But there is a method that can solve the "brain freeze" problem: journaling with prompts.

Journals with prompts take the "what do I write about" worries out of the equation, giving you specific reflection questions or directives to focus on in your writing. Often the prompts are things you'd never consider writing about on your own, so they draw out ideas and feelings that foster increased self-awareness, confidence, and personal growth you might not otherwise experience.

There are three ways to journal using this technique. You can ...

1. Buy a journal with prompts included then just respond to the daily prompt in your journal.

2. Use a blank journal, find a list of prompts online or in a book, and use them to answer questions in the blank journal. (You'll find a list of prompts further down in this section and later in the book.)

3. Create your own prompts and write them in a blank journal as soon as you purchase it. Brainstorm daily questions or topics you want to write about for the next few months or a full year if you can come up with 365 prompts.

You can never go wrong with a prompt journal because there are so many topics to choose from based on your interests, state of mind, or personal/professional goals. Steve and Barrie have created prompt journals on topics such as mindfulness, gratitude, life passions, relationships, and productivity. But you can find hundreds of options with a quick online search.

Advantages of Prompt Journaling

- Prompt journals are simple and easy. All you have to do is read and respond to each of the prompts.

- Prompt journals help you know yourself better. Many prompts will ask you to dig deep and be honest about different aspects of your life.

- There are a multitude of options. You can use prompt journals to explore and expand many areas of your life.

Disadvantages of Prompt Journaling

- Some prompts might not apply to you, or you might think they're silly. If you get enough of these questions, you'll start to feel that journaling is a waste of your time.

- The prompts can become repetitive if the topics in the journal are limited. You might end up answering the same questions over and over. The trick is to buy a journal that has plenty of engaging and unique prompts.

Who Is It For?

- A prompt journal might work best for ...

- Anyone who struggles with what to write about daily. Using a prompt is the perfect remedy, as you won't suffer from "blank page syndrome" wondering what to write about next.

- Anyone who enjoys variety and exploring different aspects of themselves by answering questions or responding to a directive.

- Anyone who prefers to be guided through the journaling experience rather than going it alone with little or no structure.

How to Get Started

1. Select the type of prompt journal that best suits you.

Decide whether you want a journal that is printed with prompts or a blank journal or notebook to copy or create your own prompts. Printed journals with prompts come in a wide variety of sizes with hardback, paperback, or spiral bound covers. They range in price from around $10.00 to over $25.00 on Amazon, depending on the size, paper quality, print color, design, and binding of the journal.

2. Keep your prompt journal where you will write in it.

Some prompt journals are small enough that you can carry them in your purse, pocket, or briefcase. But many of these journals are larger because they have more space for writing and more pages due to the number of prompts. Since you won't be writing daily or hourly activities in your journal, it doesn't need to go everywhere with you. Put it where you can easily see it after your trigger habit, or keep it in the special space or room where you've decided to do your journaling. Just be sure you have a trigger and a reminder set to write in it daily.

3. Approach prompt journaling mindfully.

Go back to the section in this book on mindfulness and journaling, and practice the centering meditation before you write your replies to the prompts in your journal. Approach this type of journaling with an open and clear mind so you can delve into your inner world without anxiety or distraction.

4. Write with honesty and openness.

This is the best way to get the most out of prompt journaling. If a question makes you uncomfortable or pushes an emotional button, that's actually a *good thing*. It reveals where you might need to do some work on yourself. Try not to put up walls with your self-revelations. Honesty and vulnerability in your writing will lead to awareness, growth, and inner healing.

Prompt Journal Topics to Consider

Here are some ideas for daily journaling with prompts. As you develop the journaling habit, it's important to write daily so you make the habit automatic. Once it is, you can back off if you wish and write every other day or a few days a week.

Inspirational Quotes

Everyone has something that inspires them to do their best in life, and inspirational quotes can serve as thought-provoking prompts for journal writing. Many journals have quotes already chosen and printed for you. But you can choose your own to write about and the deeper meaning it reflects for your life.

Self-Questions

Questions are excellent writing prompts as they naturally invite contemplation and reflection. Questions arise naturally in day-to-day life, and we rarely have time to stop and think about them in the moment, but you can write them down to journal about later. Or you may have deep, philosophical questions you want to hash out in your journal. (Check out these 101 break-through questions from Barrie's blog for ideas.[54])

Relationship Questions

If you and your spouse or partner are seeking to improve your relationship, a prompt journal with relationship questions can help you strengthen your bond and address areas of conflict. You can journal individually about your relationship or work together as a couple to answer questions and share your thoughts.

---

54 https://liveboldandbloom.com/06/self-awareness-2/
questions-to-ask-yourself

Self-Care

If you want to improve your mental, physical, or emotional well-being, you can journal about self-care practices and changes you need to make to improve your happiness and health. Or you can use a question journal to assess where you need more self-care. Just writing about self-care can make you feel better about yourself and help you release anxious or stressful feelings. (If you get stuck, Steve has 275 self-care ideas on his blog at https://www.developgoodhabits.com/self-care-ideas/.)

Life Milestones

If you have big goals you want to focus on, like graduating from college, getting married, having your first child, or buying your first home, you can write about these milestones and your plans for reaching them in a prompt journal. This type of journal is an excellent tool to help you clarify the steps required to reach your goals.

Captured Moments

If you have already reached major milestones in your life, you can write journal entries about those events. This could be a detailed recollection of your wedding day, the feeling you had when your child was born, your experience at a big event you attended, or a simple but profound moment from your day.

Finding Your Passion

Journaling prompts can help you uncover more about yourself— your personality, skills, interests, values, and intelligence type. With the right questions, a passion journal can lead you toward the work or avocation that is your calling. These questions can also help you address limiting beliefs, fears, and confusion that are holding you back.

Life Challenges

If you encounter daily struggles or one big life challenge (like an illness or death) that is particularly difficult for you, your daily journal is the perfect place to write about it. Describe in detail the struggle you are facing. What happened? How do you feel? Are you able to meet and overcome the challenges you are facing? How are you learning from them?

Define Solutions to Challenges

Write about possible solutions and action steps to help you cope with your challenges. Think about all the options you might have and how they might improve the situation. You can also write about ways the situation could have been prevented in the first place.

Write Down Prayers

If you pray daily, you can write down your prayers to increase your spiritual activity. These prayers can focus on any aspect of your spiritual life, from gratitude to praise and worship. You will find many prayer journals with printed prompts, or you can find a daily prayer or devotional online to inspire your writing.

Express Gratitude

Keeping a gratitude journal is one of the best ways to improve your attitude about life and increase your optimism. Each night, take the time to write about a few things that occurred during the day that you are grateful for. If you start writing down your blessings, you will find you have an endless number of reasons to focus on the good in your life rather than the bad.

Gratitude is such a strong thing to write about that you may want to consider having a journal specifically for expressing gratitude. It may sound odd, but writing about how you appreciate others, even if you never show anyone, actually makes you feel a lot better about yourself. (We discuss gratitude journaling in more detail later on in this chapter.)

Chronicle Your Meditation Practice

If you meditate daily, you can chronicle your journey with meditation in a journal. Write about the type of meditation you practiced, how you felt during the meditation, the challenges you experienced, and the improvements you are making.

Record Daily Memories

Your prompt can be the same every day: What do I want to remember that I saw, experienced, or learned today? By using this daily prompt, you'll create a book full of memories that will inspire you and renew positive feelings for years to come. It can be a testament to your personal or professional growth over the years.

Overcome Fears

Learning to manage and overcome worry and fear will help you release the negative feelings that hold you back and give you more confidence and motivation. Writing down your fears will help you navigate them and create plans to solve your issues in productive ways. You can purchase worry or anxiety journals with reflections, exercises, and prompts to guide you, or you can create your own questions related to your fears and concerns.

Recall Your Dreams

We all dream at night, but it's often hard to remember what we dream about. If you write down your dreams as soon as you wake up, you'll be able to reflect on them to understand the deeper meaning and explore the emotions your dreams stimulate. Dream journals with prompts can provide questions and directives that invite you to better understand the power of your dreams.

Mindfulness Journaling

Using a mindfulness journal, you can explore daily experiences with more presence and intention. Each day you can focus on a different experience, no matter how simple or mundane, in which you brought your full attention to the experience.

Many mindfulness journals have different prompts to guide your mindfulness actions. If you don't want something quite so structured, you can simply ask yourself every day, "How was I mindful today?" (Again, we will go into more detail on mindfulness journaling later in this chapter.)

Kindness Journaling

Create or purchase a prompt journal that focuses on kindness— this means writing about how people were kind to you and how you showed kindness to others. These journals help you explore the value of kindness and how it enriches and inspires your life. In a culture that has become increasingly unkind and vitriolic, kindness journaling has become more valuable than ever.

Affirmation Journaling

Use positive affirmations as a guide for your daily journal writing. Choose a different affirmation each day, write about how you are applying it in your life, and explore what it means for you. Or you can have one affirmation for each week and write about how this affirmation helps you over the next seven days. Check out the list of 101 positive affirmations[55] on Barrie's blog to get started.

Productivity Journaling

Every day you can write down your priority goal for the day and journal about how you achieved it. Your prompt will be the goal you set first thing in the morning. Then in the evening, you can write about what you did that day to make it happen.

Happiness Journaling

You can find a variety of happiness journals with prompts to help you explore what makes you happy, how to find more happiness, and actions you can take to sustain happiness. Or you can simply use the daily prompt, "What made me happy today?" and write about each experience in detail.

Creative Writing

If you want to develop your writing skills and creative thinking, you can get a journal with writing prompts that invite you to write about different scenarios, stories, or concepts. Every day, you'll have a unique prompt that stretches your imagination and allows you to write about a wide variety of topics. Check out Authority Pub's blog post for a good list[56] of journaling prompts for writers.

Self-Discovery Journaling

One of the best ways to learn more about yourself, your inner

---

55 https://liveboldandbloom.com/09/quotes/positive-affirmations
56 https://authority.pub/daily-journal-prompts/

wisdom, your hopes and dreams, and your limitations is through self-discovery journaling. The prompts in this kind of journal can be questions, or they can be the beginning of a sentence that you complete. For example, a prompt might be, "If I had a mission statement for my life, it would be ..."

Monthly Themes

If you cannot come up with a specific idea, think about themes that are present during each month of the year. In January, you can write about new beginnings. In February, love is always in the air. In June, you can write about the expectation of summer. And in October, you can talk about the autumn season.

Confidence and Self-Esteem Journaling

The prompts in this journal will focus on exploring where you are lacking in confidence and self-esteem and actions you can take to improve in these areas. You might have writing exercises to shift your focus from the things going wrong in your life to things that are going well. As you write about these issues, you'll find your confidence and self-esteem improving.

Nature Journaling

With a nature journal, your prompt might be, "What did I experience or notice in nature today?" This type of journal encourages you to get outside and notice the beauty of the natural world, both minute and majestic. Your writing will be focused on descriptions, emotional experiences, and inspiration you find from nature.

Automatic Writing

Barrie kept a journal for many years with the daily prompt, "What do I need to know today?" Then she would just write in stream of consciousness in answer to this question. You can practice this automatic writing with one prompt that you use every day, or come up with different questions or prompts to inspire your stream of consciousness writing.

Resources

You can find prompt journals on almost any subject. One strategy we suggest is to go on Amazon and tailor a search to a specific outcome you'd like to achieve. If you're looking for a goals-related journal, for example, search for "goals journal." If you'd like a few suggestions, both Barrie and Steve have published the following prompt journals:

- *The 90-Day Gratitude Journal*[57]
- *The Mindfulness Journal*[58]
- *201 Relationship Question Journal*[59]
- *The Life Passion Journal*[60]
- *3 Things A Day*[61]

---

57 https://www.amazon.com/dp/1946159158/ref=sspa_dk_detail_2?psc=1
58 https://www.amazon.com/Mindfulness-Journal-Practices-Writing-Reflections/dp/1973531690/ref=sr_1_3?ie=UTF8&qid=1537213563&sr=8-3&keywords=the+mindfulness+journal
59 https://www.amazon.com/201-Relationship-Questions-Journal-Emotional/dp/1732035008/ref=sr_1_3?ie=UTF8&qid=1537213535&sr=8-3&keywords=201+relationship+questions
60 https://www.amazon.com/Life-Passion-Journal-Self-Doubt-Remarkable/dp/1732035016/ref=sr_1_1?ie=UTF8&qid=1537213045&sr=8-1&keywords=life+passion+journal
61 https://www.amazon.com/Things-Day-Minimalist-Journal-Stress/dp/1732035040/ref=sr_1_1?ie=UTF8&qid=1537213433&sr=8-1&keywords=3+things+a+day+journal

3: Morning Pages

Working with the morning pages, we begin to sort through the differences between our real feelings, which are often secret, and our official feelings, those on the record for public display.

　　—Julia Cameron

One of the most well-loved and popular forms of journaling comes from Julia Cameron, an American teacher, author, artist, poet, playwright, novelist, filmmaker, composer, and journalist. With these impressive credentials attached to her name, it's not surprising that Cameron's international bestselling book is called, *The Artist's Way: A Spiritual Path to Higher Creativity.*[62]

In *The Artist's Way*, Cameron invites her readers and fellow creatives on a 12-week journey to "discover the inextricable link between their spiritual and creative selves," as she explains in her book description. Part of that self-discovery comes through a practice she has coined "Morning Pages," a journaling activity that has become a beloved ritual for thousands of people worldwide.

On her website,[63] she describes Morning Pages as follows:

> *Morning Pages are three pages of longhand, stream of consciousness writing, done first thing in the morning. *There is no wrong way to do Morning Pages*– they are not high art. They are not even "writing." They are about anything and everything that crosses your mind– and they are for your eyes only. Morning Pages provoke, clarify, comfort, cajole, prioritize and synchronize the day at hand. Do not over-think Morning*

62　https://www.amazon.com/Artists-Way-25th-Anniversary/dp/0143129252/ ref=sr_1_1?ie=UTF8&qid=1537213760&sr=8-1&keywords=the+artists+way

63　https://juliacameronlive.com/basic-tools/morning-pages/

Pages: just put three pages of anything on the page ... and then do three more pages tomorrow.

The idea here is to pour out all the thoughts and emotions rattling around your head—anger, fear, anxiety, jealousy, and self-doubt. And this must be done first thing in the morning, according to Julia Cameron's directive.

Your goal is to get it out on paper so it doesn't show up in your personal and professional life.

As Cameron says, "When people ask, 'Why do we write Morning Pages?' I joke, 'To get to the other side.' They think I am kidding, but I'm not. Morning Pages do get us to the other side: the other side of our fear, our negativity, of our moods."

The beauty of Morning Pages is the simplicity of the style and the freedom to write whatever comes to mind, no matter how silly, strange, or unimportant the words seem at the time. This mental purging unlocks pent-up emotions and negative thoughts without resistance or self-judgment—or judgment from others.

Advantages of Morning Pages

- Often, the biggest solution to your problem requires a bit of deep digging, and Morning Pages helps you tap into your subconscious. Because the writing is stream of consciousness, and you are writing so much, you can learn a lot about yourself.

- Morning Pages are cathartic, allowing you to release pent-up emotions. This improves your mental health and overall well-being.

- Morning Pages require daily consistency, which helps you

build the journaling habit and boost your writing skills, creativity, and mindfulness.

Disadvantages of Morning Pages

- They can be time-consuming. Three pages of writing can take 30 to 60 minutes to complete. For some, this is too much of a time commitment.

- Morning Pages can be too intense or emotional for some. While you might find writing Morning Pages can be cathartic, you may not be prepared for some of the emotions that arise from stream of consciousness writing.

Who Is It For?

Morning Pages might work best for ...

- Anyone who is a creative and feels stuck with their work or life.

- Anyone who wants to bring clarity to their thinking and unlock new ideas.

- Anyone who wants to tap into their intuition and subconscious mind.

- Anyone who wants to feel less stress and anxiety.

How to Get Started

1. Don't worry about rules.

There is no wrong way to write your Morning Pages. Write whatever comes to your mind. Write about what you see in your room. Write the same words over and over. The important thing is that you write.

2. Choose your Morning Pages journal.

A notebook is perfectly fine for Morning Pages, but you can also choose a decorative journal that has lined or blank pages. Letter-size pages are optimal.

3. Wake up 30 minutes earlier than normal.

You'll need the extra time in the morning to write your pages. Give your subconscious mind a nudge by telling yourself the night before that you will get up 30 minutes earlier and feel well-rested when you awaken. This reminder really helps.

4. Always write in the morning.

Julia Cameron makes a big deal about this—otherwise she would have called them the "Any-Time-of-Day Pages." The morning is when you are still closest to sleep, and your ego hasn't had time to interfere with your subconscious mind. You'll be more honest and open, less likely to censor your writing.

5. Foster a positive mental attitude.

Rather than thinking, "Oh crap, I have to write these stupid pages," begin your day with a statement (mental or verbal) like, "This is going to be a great day." Put yourself in a positive frame of mind before writing.

6. Write three full pages in longhand.

Three pages is about 750 words on letter-size paper. If you're writing in a small notebook, don't shortchange yourself. Use the 750-word guide to get the most out of your effort.

7. Don't get ahead of yourself.

If you think about how you have to write three pages tomorrow and the day after that, you'll sour your motivation before you develop the habit. Just think about the pages you are writing this morning. Tomorrow you can think about that day's pages.

8. Have your tools ready the night before.

Put your notebook and pen on your bedside table if you plan to write in bed or next to the chair or table in your room where you write. Try not to leave your bedroom to write, or you might get distracted by something else. Complete your writing before you take a shower, get your coffee, or otherwise start your day.

9. Expect some morning brain fog at first.

If you're still sleepy, your first few paragraphs of writing might not make much sense. That's fine. The more you write, the more your synapses will start firing, and you'll find your writing flows. If it doesn't, just write, "I don't know what to write," until something comes to you.

10. Refrain from judging your Morning Pages.

This is true for any type of journaling but especially important for Morning Pages. This is free flow writing that isn't meant to "make sense" or have any particular structure. Don't undermine the experience by judging it.

Resources

Here are some resources to inspire you with Morning Pages journaling:

- *The Artist's Way: A Spiritual Path to Higher Creativity*[64]
- The Artist's Way Morning Pages Journal[65]
- 750 Words.[66] If you don't mind creating a digital version of Morning Pages, you can use this tool to create a private version of your Morning Pages. It allows you t0 track various metrics related to the pages such as typing speed, total words, consecutive days, etc.

---

64 https://www.amazon.com/Artists-Way-25th-Anniversary-
ebook/dp/B006H19H3M/ref=sr_1_3?ie=UTF8&qid=1535740416
&sr=8-3&keywords=the+artist+way

65 https://www.amazon.com/Artists-Way-Morning-Pages-
Journal/dp/0143129414/ref=sr_1_6?ie=UTF8&qid=1535740416
&sr=8-6&keywords=the+artist+way

66 **http://750words.com/**

4: Mindfulness Journaling

The best way to capture moments is to pay attention. This is how we cultivate mindfulness.

—Jon Kabat-Zinn

We mentioned mindfulness journaling earlier, but we feel it is so valuable that it deserves a section of its own. Multiple studies[67] confirm how powerful and life changing the daily practice of mindfulness is.

It has been shown to reduce rumination and overthinking; alleviate stress; improve memory, concentration, and performance; help with emotional reactivity; improve sleep; boost creativity; improve relationship happiness; and provide pain relief.

If you're not already a practitioner of mindfulness, or if you're not clear what mindfulness is, here's how we explain it in our book *10-Minute Mindfulness:*[68]

> *Mindfulness is very simple. It means you become intentionally aware of the present moment, while paying close attention to your feelings, thoughts, and sensations of the body.*
>
> *You pay attention on purpose, and consciously direct your awareness to whatever you are doing or thinking. Washing dishes. Talking to your spouse. Playing with your kids. Working on a project. Doing nothing.*

---

67 http://www.apa.org/monitor/2012/07-08/ce-corner.aspx

68 https://www.amazon.com/10-Minute-Mindfulness-Habits-Living-Present-ebook/dp/B071HVMVVR/ref=sr_1_1?ie=UTF8&qid=1536082503&sr=8-1&keywords=10+minute+mindfulness+71+habits+for+living+in+the+present+moment

But mindfulness involves one further step—the practice of non-judgment.

Non-judgment is the key to experiencing the deeper benefits of a daily mindfulness practice. It requires that you observe your actions, thoughts, and feelings from a distance, without labeling them as good or bad, right or wrong.

There are a variety of ways to practice mindfulness during your day—meditation, deep breathing, or spending time in nature, for example. But we consider *mindfulness journaling* to be one of the best ways to deepen the practice of presence.

Similar to Morning Pages, mindfulness journaling helps you connect with your emotions and experience the world in the here and now rather than attaching your thoughts to the past or future, where you often find negativity and anxiety.

Focused writing alone is a form of mindfulness. But a mindfulness journal allows you to explore various practices of present moment awareness and to contemplate how these practices impact your well-being.

If you are a new or even a seasoned mindfulness student, writing about your experiences with mindfulness will help you master the practice, reflect on your thoughts and experiences, and provide a permanent record of your efforts at deepening the amount of purposeful intention in your life.

There is no specific way you're supposed to write in a mindfulness journal. Unlike Morning Pages, you can write a few sentences or several pages. You can use a blank journal to chronicle and explore mindfulness on your own, or you can use a journal with prompts, like our daily journal, *The Mindfulness Journal: Daily*

Practices, Writing Prompts, and Reflections for Living in the Present Moment.[69]

Advantages of Mindfulness Journaling

- Mindfulness journaling provides all of the physical, mental, and emotional benefits previously listed.

- Mindfulness journaling reinforces your day-to-day efforts to be more present and aware.

- Mindfulness journaling increases feelings of happiness, as studies[70] show a direct correlation between happiness and mindfulness.

Disadvantages of Mindfulness Journaling

- Mindfulness journaling may be too slow or self-reflective for some journal writers.

- Mindfulness journaling may be more time-consuming than other types of journals.

Who Is It For?

Mindfulness journaling might work best for:

- People who are struggling with depression, anxiety, and stress and need an effective tool to reduce symptoms.

- Those who are seeking to enhance their mindfulness practices by writing about them.

- Those who want specific instructions on mindfulness

---

69 https://www.amazon.com/Mindfulness-Journal-Practices-Writing-Reflections/dp/1973531690/ref=sr_1_1?ie=UTF8&qid=1536082566 &sr=8-1&keywords=the+mindfulness+journal

70 http://berkeleysciencereview.com/can-mindfulness-make-you-happier/

practices with prompts that direct them to perform and then write about specific activities.

How to Get Started

1. Choose the type of mindfulness journal you want to use.

We are partial to a journal with prompts (because we created one!), but you may prefer a blank journal in which you create your own mindfulness activities to write about.

2. If you don't use a prompt journal, create your own strategy.

Decide how you want to use your journal to practice and explore mindfulness. Maybe you write about your daily meditation practice, or you write about one activity every day in which you were fully focused and present. You might write about the thoughts going through your head as you are journaling or describe the physical sensations you are experiencing in the moment.

3. Practice a short meditation before you begin.

See the instructions in the "How to Combine Journaling with Mindfulness" chapter covered earlier in this book. This practice will help you be more centered and focused as you write.

4. Go for a short walk outside, or experience nature.

This is optional, but it can give you something to write about that connects your mind to the physical world and the beauty around you.

5. Use this one daily prompt and write about it in every entry.

"In this moment, I am ..." Then just write what comes to mind.

6. Use some of the prompts below from *The Mindfulness Journal* to help you get started.

I reflect on the people in my life who have made me feel loved and supported. I feel grateful for ...

Gratitude is a mindfulness practice that opens you to joy, compassion, and appreciation of the life that sustains you. Begin your morning or end your day with contemplation on those who have made a positive impact on your life.

As I sit quietly, I notice each breath I take, following the intake of air through my nose and into my lungs, and the slow exhalation as I release the air through my nose. As I repeat this mindful breathing for several minutes, I notice my body ...

Most mindfulness practices begin with your body by drawing your attention to your breath and the quality of sensation. In ancient Buddhist teachings of "The Four Foundations of Mindfulness," the first teaching is "mindfulness of the body," which involves becoming familiar with and even being loving toward the body. Body mindfulness anchors you in the here and now.

Today I sit quietly for a few moments and observe my thoughts as they float by in my mind. I don't judge them, I just watch and notice. What does observation reveal to me about my thoughts?

Your thoughts can trigger anxiety, unhappiness, and anger, which can keep your mind trapped in a constant negative loop. This cycle happens because we are unconscious of our thoughts, and we allow them to run rampant in our brains without challenging them.

At home, I choose a routine chore (like washing dishes or folding clothes) and give my full and focused attention to every element of the chore. This is what I noticed ...

There is an opportunity for mindfulness in everything you do, in every task and seemingly unimportant activity of your day. When you align your attention and mental focus to whatever you are doing, you are truly living. You are here, now, experiencing the beauty and perfection of the moment.

As I meditate today, I notice my emotions and moods. As emotions and feelings arise, I simply name them without judgment. "This is anxiety." "This is sleepiness." In meditation today, I discovered ...

Meditation is the centerpiece of a mindfulness practice, allowing you to cultivate an attitude of compassionate indifference to your thoughts by ceasing to identify with them. During meditation, you observe the patterns of your mind and learn to tame the incessant chattering of your thoughts.

Today I visualize the following outcome and the specific actions I'll take to reach that outcome ...

Visualization is a mindfulness tool using mental imagery to help you mentally rehearse an outcome or bring about a state of relaxation. It can be used in daily life to relieve stress, enhance motivation, and add more power to your physical and mental efforts.

This morning I create a ritual around my morning cup of tea or coffee by paying full attention to all aspects of preparation, drinking, savoring, and cleaning up. This is how I celebrated my morning beverage, and how it made me feel ...

Rituals are actions we imbue with meaning and significance that enhance our lives in some way. They are performed in a prescribed way that lends an element of sacredness to the occasion, and they slow us down enough that we can connect to the present moment.

Before I eat a meal that I or someone else has prepared, I take time today to notice the food, smell the aromas, and feel gratitude for the bounty before me. Taking this moment made me feel ...

In our modern lives, there is little time to prepare, savor, and appreciate what we are eating. We become disconnected from our source of sustenance and energy. Preparing food and eating it more mindfully not only allows you to be present with the experience, but also can help you to prevent overeating, lose weight, and become more aware of your body's needs.

I spent time today being fully present and engaged with someone I care about. This is how I spent my time with him/her, and how this time together made me feel ...

Being present with someone means you are fully attentive, engaged, and focused on the other person. You aren't looking at your phone, distracted by the television, or thinking about the next thing you need to do. You are actively listening, responding, and showing with your words, expressions, and demeanor that you are completely in the moment with this person.

Today I sit outside in a quiet spot in nature. I close my eyes and take a few deep, cleansing breaths. Then I just listen. I notice all of the sounds around me. This is what I heard and experienced by listening to nature ...

The beauty and simplicity of nature is what makes it so ideally suited to practicing mindfulness. Unlike our daily lives and the hectic world around us, nature's allure is often subtle. The simple experience of walking outside in your backyard is a great opportunity to practice mindfulness.

7. Stay rooted in the present moment.

When you sit down to write, it's easy to get distracted by irrelevant things. The phone may ring, or you may get an email notification—or you could hear a siren in the background. You may start daydreaming, or you may even start to think about other things you need to do.

Here are some tips that can help you:

- Learn to accept these distractions as your passing thoughts, and label them as "thinking."

- After this happens, return to the present moment and refocus on your writing. It is natural for your mind to wander every now and then while you are working—it is just important to learn how to acknowledge it and move on.

- One great way to get these thoughts out of your head is to write them down so you know you can revisit them later.

- Take some time before you start writing to empty all of your thoughts onto paper or create a to-do list to handle at a later time. Try to focus as much as you can on your writing, and leave the other details of your life to be addressed at a later time.

8. If you get stuck, try some breathing exercises.

Breathing will help you control your "monkey mind" and the random thoughts that interrupt the flow of writing. It can also help you break the pattern of writer's block. Try a simple breathing exercise[71] to help calm and clear your mind.

Resources:

- The Mindfulness Journal[72]

---

71 https://www.mindbodygreen.com/0-4386/A-Simple-Breathing-Exercise-to-Calm-Your-Mind-Body.html

72 https://www.amazon.com/Mindfulness-Journal-Practices-Writing-Reflections/dp/1973531690

5: Gratitude Journaling

Acknowledging the good that you already have in your life is the foundation for all abundance.

   —Eckhart Tolle

Gratitude journaling is another style of mindfulness journaling. By its very nature, the feeling and expression of gratitude leaves no room for regrets about the past or worries for the future.

When you are grateful, you are anchored in the reality of your blessings in the here and now. And like other mindfulness practices, the practice of gratitude has many mental and physical benefits.

According to an article[73] in the Harvard Health Newsletter, which outlines research on the topic, "Gratitude is strongly and consistently associated with greater happiness. Gratitude helps people feel more positive emotions, relish good experiences, improve their health, deal with adversity, and build strong relationships."

American psychologist, educator, and author Martin Seligman and his team performed a study[74] in which participants were asked to write down "three good things" that occurred during their day, explaining why each item was personally important. After completing this exercise for a week, the participants reported more happiness (and less depression) at the one-month, three-month, and six-month follow-up sessions.

Says Sonja Lyubomirsky, author of *The How of Happiness: A*

---

73 https://www.health.harvard.edu/newsletter_article/in-praise-of-gratitude
74 https://www.ncbi.nlm.nih.gov/pubmed/16045394

Scientific Approach to Getting the Life You Want,[75] "Gratitude is an antidote to negative emotions, a neutralizer of envy, hostility, worry, and irritation. It is savoring; it is not taking things for granted; it is present oriented."

As a renowned researcher on happiness, Lyubomirsky advises keeping a journal in which you count your blessings or write gratitude letters to boost happiness levels. Journaling is one of the best ways to practice gratitude because you enhance your grateful feelings as you write about them. The process of writing, particularly in longhand, prolongs the experience of gratefulness.

You also create a "history of gratitude" by chronicling your daily blessings—one that you can return to again and again to renew your appreciation for life and the positive feelings gratitude inspires.

Because we are all prone to ruminate on negativity and dwell on our regrets, frustrations, and grievances, a gratitude journal is an effective and inexpensive mental health tool directing our mental energies away from destructive thoughts and toward more healing, uplifting thoughts.

If gratitude journaling appeals to you, you can find many gratitude journals with questions or prompts, like our *90-Day Gratitude Journal.*[76] Or you can use a blank journal to record your blessings using a method you devise yourself or using one of the suggestions we outline in this chapter.

---

75 https://www.amazon.com/How-Happiness-Approach-Getting-Life-ebook/dp/B0010O927W/ref=sr_1_1?ie=UTF8&qid=1536675558&sr=8-1&keywords=the+how+of+happiness

76 https://www.amazon.com/gp/product/1946159158?pf_rd_p=d1f45e03-8b73-4c9a-9beb-4819111bef9a&pf_rd_r=Y3269RJ1DRCV1AJQM35G

Advantages of Gratitude Journaling

- **Gratitude journaling increases your happiness.** When you regularly practice gratitude through journaling, you'll notice that you're flooded with feelings of abundant positivity. You'll also notice the positive things in your life that you have taken for granted in the past. When you learn to consider and appreciate these things, your levels of happiness will increase.

- **Gratitude journaling helps you cope with life challenges.** Trauma, stress, and negative life events can have the counterintuitive effect of making us feel more grateful. In his book *Thanks! How Practicing Gratitude Can Make You Happier*,[77] Dr. Robert Emmons found that in the days after the 9/11 attacks in the United States, gratitude was the second most commonly felt emotion after sympathy. Journaling about the good things in your life, even when bad things are happening, will help you better cope with the bad things.

- **Gratitude journaling improves relationships.** We often take for granted the people closest to us. Their habits and behaviors annoy us, and we tend to focus on their negative qualities rather than the qualities we love about them. Writing about the positive traits of your loved ones and why you love them so much will make your relationships happier and more rewarding.

---

77 https://www.amazon.com/Thanks-Practicing-Gratitude-Make-Happier/dp/0547085737/ref=sr_1_1?ie=UTF8&qid=1536676008&sr=8-1&keywords=Thanks%21+How+Practicing+Gratitude+Can+Make+You+Happier

Disadvantages of Gratitude Journaling

- **Gratitude journaling can feel false if you are deeply unhappy.** You might approach this type of journaling with cynicism if you are depressed or so unhappy that you can't focus on anything except your difficult emotions. You won't be likely to stick with it if expressing gratitude feels disingenuous.

- **Gratitude journaling about toxic people isn't productive.** We all have negative qualities, but some people are so difficult or toxic that conjuring up feelings of gratitude about them is more detrimental than helpful. You could be putting a Band-Aid on an issue that needs to be tackled head-on. Instead of trying to "find the good" in this person, perhaps you should be looking for ways to end this relationship.

Who Is It For?

Gratitude journaling might work best for ...

- Anyone who is prone to ruminating or frequently experiences negativity. You can use gratitude to retrain your automatic thinking so you focus more on the positive aspects of your life.

- Those who want to better appreciate their blessings and make time to savor them more thoroughly and mindfully.

- People who are experiencing life difficulties or a serious challenge to help them refocus their attention on the aspects of their lives that are good and fulfilling.

How to Get Started

1. Choose the type of gratitude journal you want to use.

There are a variety of gratitude journals with prompts and for different audiences (men, women, Christians, etc.) you can find on Amazon ranging in price from about $10.00 to over $20.00. Some cover shorter periods of time, and others provide room to write for a full year or longer. Some are one line a day or bullet journals, and others give you more space to write longer entries. Decide how much gratitude writing you want to do in a day by looking at these various styles. You can also choose a blank or lined journal to create your own gratitude strategy.

2. Create a ritual around gratitude journaling.

You can make it more of a mindfulness activity by ritualizing your efforts. Consider some or all of the following activities before you start writing:

- Playing a favorite song
- Lighting a candle
- Drinking a cup of tea
- Taking a relaxing bath
- Saying a calming prayer
- Meditating before you begin

3. Be as specific as possible with your gratitude descriptions.

In our journal, *The 90-Day Gratitude Journal*, we recommend two daily prompts to help you pinpoint exactly what makes you feel grateful. Here's an excerpt from our journal to explain these two prompts.

Question 1: "I am grateful for ____, because ____."

This statement is based on a study by Martin Seligman that confirmed that the best way to express gratitude is to not only describe what you're grateful for, but also to take the time to consider the actions that led to this good result. When you start to see a positive correlation between your actions and certain events, you'll do more to attract these good things into your life.

The purpose here is to challenge you to be ultra-specific about what you're *currently* grateful for. This means you'll describe how a person, event, or item has benefited your life, and in what ways you have been helped.

There are many things to be grateful for:

- *Specific people in your life.* Even with someone who annoys or angers you, there is always a lesson to be learned from every interaction you have with others.

- *Certain possessions.* You can journal about items that have enriched your life or made it better in some way.

- *Things you take for granted.* There are many people, possessions, or conditions in your life right now that you might take for granted—like your health, job, relationships, or even a piece of technology. A great way to express gratitude is to recognize how your life would be different if you didn't have one of these specific items.

- *Random surprises.* One of the best ways to feel grateful is by taking the time to recognize unexpected, positive events that occur.

- *Small moments.* Sometimes the best things to be grateful for are everyday experiences: Playing with your children. A warm summer day. The taste of your favorite beverage. Taking time to appreciate these moments will help you value every single experience.

We challenge you to come up with a unique answer for every day you journal. That way, you'll have an ongoing list of all the items and people that have added value to your existence. You can then review this journal whenever you feel the need for an emotional boost.

Question 2: "What am I looking forward to today (or tomorrow)?"

This question should be easy to answer.

If you're journaling in the morning, write down one thing that you're looking forward to doing by the end of the day. It could be spending time with someone important, working on a fun project, or simply relaxing at the end of the day.

If you prefer to journal in the evening, journal about something you're excited about for tomorrow.

Don't overthink your response here. Just pick one thing that will be wonderful about the next 24 hours.

4. Turn negatives into positives.

If you have something upsetting or challenging going on in your life, look for something positive you can dwell on that reduces the pain or frustration. For example, you might say, "I'm upset that relationship didn't work out, but now I have time to focus on myself and figure out what I really want and need in a partner.

5. Journal before bed to close your day on a positive note.

This will help you release anxiety, stress, or negative thinking before you fall asleep. Also, when you journal at night, you have the full day to dwell on and consider all the blessings you encountered throughout the day.

6. Follow these researched-based tips for keeping a gratitude journal[78]

(from Robert Emmons, the world's leading scientific expert on gratitude and professor of psychology at UC Davis).

- **Don't just go through the motions.** Research by psychologist Sonja Lyubomirsky and others suggests that journaling is more effective if you first make the conscious decision to become happier and more grateful. "Motivation to become happier plays a role in the efficacy of journaling," says Emmons.

- **Go for depth over breadth.** Elaborating in detail about a particular thing for which you're grateful carries more benefits than a superficial list of many things.

- **Get personal.** Focusing on people to whom you are grateful has more of an impact than focusing on things for which you are grateful.

- **Try subtraction, not just addition.** One effective way of stimulating gratitude is to reflect on what your life would be like without certain blessings, rather than just tallying up all those good things.

---

78 http://ei.yale.edu/what-is-gratitude/

- **Savor surprises.** Try to record events that were unexpected or surprising, as these tend to elicit stronger levels of gratitude.

Resources

- *The 90-Day Gratitude Journal*[79]

---

79 https://www.amazon.com/gp/product/1946159158?pf_rd_p=d1f45e03-8b73-4c9a-9beb-4819111bef9a&pf_rd_r=Y3269RJ1DRCV1AJQM35G

6: Idea Journaling

All achievements, all earned riches, have their beginning in an idea.
  —Napoleon Hill

Your brain is full of great ideas that often come to you at the most inopportune times—in the shower, on a run, or just as you're falling asleep. Before you have a chance to capture them, they evaporate into the mist of your memory, leaving you with that frustrated feeling of having missed an opportunity.

But what if you were more intentional about your ideas? What if you took the time to brainstorm and write down your ideas before they floated out of your mind?

Many famous people, like Leonardo da Vinci, Marie Curie, Beatrix Potter, and Thomas Edison, kept idea journals to stimulate their creativity and capture moments of inspiration. These musings resulted in breathtaking works of art and architecture, Nobel Prize–winning research, beloved children's stories, and world-altering inventions.

An idea journal is essential for anyone who wants to turn their own musings into reality. It's a private place to seed ideas and watch them grow—to jot down daily goals, big goals, aha moments, observations, and inspiration. It's also a good place to tease out an idea to determine how to take it from a concept to a series of actions that lead to a result.

American hedge fund manager, entrepreneur, bestselling author, venture capitalist, and podcaster, James Altucher, says, "Ideas are the currency of life. Not money. Money gets depleted until you go broke. But good ideas buy you good experiences, buy you better ideas, buy you better experiences, buy you more time, save your life."

Altucher writes about his own system[80] for generating ideas by brainstorming and writing down ten ideas a day with the main purpose of simply "exercising your idea muscle."

These could be ten business ideas, ten ideas for improving your marriage, ten new chapters for your book, or just ten random ideas that arise spontaneously. They don't have to be great ideas or even actionable ideas. Like Morning Pages writing, the point is to just brainstorm and write.

Ten ideas a day will turn into 3,650 ideas a year. There's a good chance that at least a few of these golden idea nuggets can transform your life.

Steve keeps a small journal with him at all times to capture ideas that may arise randomly. He also uses this journal to jot down ideas for his books, online businesses, and challenges he's experiencing in his personal life. In fact, almost everything he's published has started out as an entry in this journal.

You can find idea journals with prompts and instructions, but we think the best type of journal for ideas and brainstorming is a blank or lined journal. If you want to exercise your idea muscle, you need to generate the ideas yourself.

Advantages of Idea Journaling

- Idea journaling enhances creativity, analytical thinking, prioritizing, and focus.
- Idea journaling can accelerate your career and income,

---

80 https://jamesaltucher.com/2014/05/
the-ultimate-guide-for-becoming-an-idea-machine/

especially if you're in a career where your ideas can be profitable (such as writers, creatives, entrepreneurs, and professionals).

- Idea journaling is a "keystone" habit, one that motivates you to take action on other habits or goals. As you write down ideas, you'll be more likely to see them to fruition.

Disadvantages of Idea Journaling

- Idea journaling can be challenging as a daily habit if you are using it only to brainstorm solutions to problems or challenges that have a limited timeframe. The best way to make it a regular practice is by following James Altucher's advice to write down ideas every day on a variety of topics.

- Idea journaling can be frustrating if you can't implement any of your ideas. You may need to change the type of ideas you write about to those that are actionable in the near future. For example, if you brainstorm ideas for a new business, but you can't start a new business for financial or other reasons, it may agitate and disappoint you. Instead, write down ideas for earning extra money or changing your situation to set the foundation for a new business venture.

Who Is It For?

Idea journaling might work best for ...

- Anyone who wants to exercise their idea muscle and enhance their creativity.

- Creatives, writers, entrepreneurs, and professionals whose careers rely on producing profitable ideas.

How to Get Started

1. Choose the type of journal you want to use.

It can be a notebook or any type of blank or lined journal with room for jotting down ideas. If you're more of a bullet point idea person, a smaller journal that fits in your purse or pocket works just fine. James Altucher uses a server's pad (yes, the one waitstaff at restaurants use). Steve uses a small Moleskine. However, if you prefer to write longer sentences and flesh out ideas as you generate them, you might consider a bigger journal with more space.

2. Determine a block of time for brainstorming and writing.

We suggest you start with ten minutes, setting a timer to keep you on track. Steve uses aTimeLogger[81] to track his work block, including his journaling efforts.

3. Stick to a set number of ideas for each session.

James Altucher recommends ten ideas because it forces your "brain to sweat." Most of us can crank out four or five ideas pretty quickly, but coming up with the remainder is more difficult. If you find that generating ten ideas in ten minutes is too hard, reduce the number of ideas but still write enough to create that brain sweat.

4. Write your own unique prompt for each session.

You might start with ideas related to your personal life or a personal challenge you are experiencing that requires a solution. Some examples might be:

- 10 Ways to Make Extra Money

81 http://www.atimelogger.com/

- 10 Careers that Might Interest You
- 10 Ways to Show Your Spouse You Love Her
- 10 Interests or Hobbies You Can Monetize
- 10 Ways You Can Advance Your Career
- 10 Weekend Getaways to Enjoy with Your Family

5. Avoid perfectionism or judging your ideas.

You can decide later if your ideas are worth pursuing. Just focus on getting your thoughts on paper rather than analyzing the quality of the idea or whether or not you should implement it.

6. Revisit your ideas to create goals.

Once a week, go through your list to identify ideas that might have merit. Clarify the first step you need to take to put this idea into action. In the next section, we'll review goal journaling to help you flesh out your ideas and turn them into actionable goals.

Resources

- Moleskine notebook[82]
- Server's Pad[83]
- Evernote[84]

---

82 https://www.amazon.com/
Moleskine-Classic-Notebook-Sketching-Journaling/dp/8883701127
83 https://www.amazon.com/
restaurant-Waitress-optimized-confident-detachable/dp/B07BZR4L6N
84 https://www.evernote.com

7: Goal Journaling

By recording your dreams and goals on paper, you set in motion the process of becoming the person you most want to be. Put your future in good hands—your own.
　　—Mark Victor Hansen

Are you working on a big goal, or do you frequently have smaller goals that you're pursuing? If so, you might want to create the habit of *goal journaling*. In fact, we believe goal journaling is valuable for everyone, because we all want to achieve something, and putting that something down on paper makes it more real and attainable.

Just listing out your goals is good, but journaling about them takes it a step further. Goal journaling helps you delve deeper into yourself, your dreams, and your ambitions. The more you expound on your goals, the easier it is to brainstorm action steps and solutions to manifest them.

Writing about big vision, long-term goals as well as the more immediate but smaller goals are both valuable aspects of goal journaling. However, our short-term goals can overtake all of our time and energy because they are often related to the demands of our personal and professional lives.

With long-term goals, you must be more intentional, carving out the time to set them, explore them, and implement them. A goal journal invites you to explore these visionary goals and keeps you on track so you don't ignore them.

Whether you're creating bigger, long-term goals or listing out more immediate goals, you need to begin with the big picture—the outcome you want to achieve. Then you can drill down to the smaller milestones you need to reach and the daily and weekly action steps to keep you moving toward your goals.

Journaling about your goals can help you accomplish so many things, such as:

- Finding a new career
- Losing weight
- Getting out of debt
- Decluttering your house
- Finishing a big project
- Starting a new business
- Increasing your income
- Improving your marriage
- Learning a new skill
- Traveling the world
- Being involved with your children
- Building your dream home
- Running a marathon
- Getting a degree
- Writing a book
- Starting a podcast
- Improving your public speaking skills
- Being more socially responsible
- Moving to a new city

You can find goal journals that offer prompts, space for writing daily tasks and deadlines, and motivational quotes, ranging from around $8.00 to over $20.00. Or you can purchase a blank or lined notebook to use as your goals journal.

There are also goal-setting apps like GoalsOnTrack[85] or Coach. me.[86] Both of these apps are free on iOS and Android phones, and both have journaling features.

Advantages of Goal Journaling

- Goal journaling helps you stay committed to your goals. By writing them down, exploring them, and examining the reason why you are setting them, you become more attached to them. When you write down the action steps to achieve them, you are more likely to follow through.

- Goal journaling helps you overcome challenges. We all experience the occasional obstacle. So instead of giving up when things get difficult, you can use journaling to write down potential solutions and then test them.

- Goal journaling provides a template for other goals. All goals follow a similar set of repeatable steps. So once you've used goal journaling to achieve a major goal, you can repeat this process for others.

Disadvantages of Goal Journaling

- Goal journaling can be repetitive. If your goal requires the same actions over and over (like losing weight and sticking to a budget), the process of journaling your experiences can get boring after a few weeks. There are only so many ways you can describe the actions you need to take daily.

---

85 https://www.goalsontrack.com/
86 http://coach.me

Who Is It For?

Goal journaling might work best for ...

- Anyone who has a major goal that requires 100% focus. Whether it's to lose weight, build a business, or get out of debt, we all have those goals that can have a huge impact on our lives. So journaling about it daily can help keep it at the top of your mind and become an invaluable tool as you write about your experiences.

- Anyone who tends to put off setting goals. Most of us have goals, but we often neglect to act on them. We get busy and distracted and don't carve out the time to work on our goals. A goal journal serves as a daily reminder to take action on your goals.

How to Get Started

1. Choose the type of journal you want to use.

If you prefer more of a free form style of writing about your goals and creating action items, then a blank or lined notebook will work just fine. You may prefer more direction and guidance with your goals. If so, try a journal with prompts or directive formatting or a goals app that keeps you on track.

2. Write down the big picture goal you want to achieve.

But state your goal as an intention rather than just a list item. For example, if you want to run a marathon, you would write, "I intend to run a marathon." An *intention* has an element of conviction and determination attached to it that will motivate you to achieve your goal.

3. Examine your "why."

Defining the reason why you want to achieve a goal gives you more motivation and inspiration to make it happen. Why do you want to improve your marriage? Because you love your spouse, you know it will make you both happier and healthier, and you know it will make your children feel more secure.

4. Rewrite your goal as a S.M.A.R.T. goal.

George T. Doran, a consultant and former Director of Corporate Planning for Washington Water Power Company, created and detailed the acronym in a 1981 article for *Management Review*. The acronym stands for: **S**pecific, **M**easurable, **A**ttainable, **R**elevant, and **T**ime-bound. Let's review each of these.

Specific

Specific goals answer six "W" questions: "Who?," "What?," "Where?," "When?," "Which?," and "Why?".

When you can identify each element, you'll know which tools (and actions) are required to reach a goal:

- Who is involved?
- What do you want to accomplish?
- Where will you complete the goal?
- When do you want to do it?
- Which requirements and constraints might get in your way?
- Why are you doing it? (As we mentioned in step 3 above.)

Specificity is important because when you reach these

milestones (date, location, and objective), you'll know for certain you have achieved your goal.

Measurable

Measurable goals are defined with precise times, amounts, or other units—essentially, anything that measures progress toward a goal.

Creating measurable goals makes it easy to determine if you have progressed from point A to point B.

Measurable goals also help you figure out when you're headed in the right direction and when you're not. A measurable goal statement answers questions starting with "How," such as "How much?," "How many?," and "How fast?".

Attainable

Attainable goals stretch the limits of what you think is possible. While they're not impossible to complete, they're often challenging and full of obstacles.

The key to creating an attainable goal is to look at your current life and set an objective that seems *slightly* beyond your reach. That way, even if you fail, you still accomplish something of significance.

Relevant

Relevant goals focus on what you truly desire and what is going on in your personal or professional life. They are the exact opposite of inconsistent or scattered goals.

They are in harmony with everything that is important in

your life, from success in your career to happiness with the people you love.

Time-Bound

Time-bound goals have specific deadlines. You are expected to achieve your desired outcome before a target date. Time-bound goals are challenging and grounding.

You can set your target date for today, or you can set it for a few months, a few weeks, or a few years from now. The key to creating a time-bound goal is to set a deadline you'll meet by working backward and developing habits (more on this later).

5. Focus on specific milestones for your goal.

This is where journaling comes in. For each week (or ten days), create a small milestone that moves you closer to your main goal. List all of the tasks or action steps required to reach that milestone. You can assign each task to a specific day during the week you're working toward the milestone.

6. Write down MITs (most important tasks).

It's easy to feel overwhelmed if you start the day with a to-do list full of tasks, appointments, and projects. You can simplify your list by identifying the tasks that have the biggest impact on your career or life and do them first thing in the morning. Our suggestion is to pick one to three MITs that absolutely must be completed by the end of the day.

7. Journal about your personal thoughts.

These should be kept separate from the list of actions you need to complete. Your main content should stay concise, but you can reserve additional space in your journal for your own input, feelings, and ideas. You can write about:

- Specific steps you want to test
- Limiting beliefs and negative thoughts you're experiencing
- Resources (books, podcasts, websites) that might help you learn more about your goal
- Challenges you're currently experiencing
- Ideas and solutions to these obstacles

8. Conduct a weekly review of your goal work.

This review will be longer than your typical daily journaling session. Go over each of your weekly goals and ask three simple questions:

- What went right? Celebrate the small victories you've achieved and what you did well that week.
- What went wrong? Identify the obstacles and setbacks you encountered.
- What's my action plan? Create a S.M.A.R.T. goal for the next week and write down what you'll do to achieve it.

9. Date all your entries.

Be sure to write down the date every time you write in your goal journal. This will help you keep track of when you completed items, what you've achieved during a journaling session, and how consistent you've been with writing in your journal.

10. Celebrate your achievements.

When you complete a goal, do something to celebrate what you've accomplished. Reward yourself with something that feels special or a purchase you've been putting off until you achieved your goal. Then write about your reward in your goal journal.

Resources

- BestSelf Co.'s The Self Journal[87] (Amazon)[88]
- BestSelf Co.'s Project Action Pad[89]
- BestSelf Co.'s Weekly Action Pad[90]
- Barrie Davenport's *3 Things A Day Journal: A Minimalist Journal for More Focus with Less Stress*[91]
- The Freedom Journal[92]

---

87 https://bestself.co/collections/all/products/self-journal

88 https://www.amazon.com/BestSelf-Co-SELF-Journal-Productivity/dp/B01MS263H1/

89 https://bestself.co/collections/all/products/project-action-pad

90 https://bestself.co/collections/all/products/weekly-action-planner

91 https://www.amazon.com/Things-Day-Minimalist-Journal-Stress/dp/1732035040

92 https://www.developgoodhabits.com/the-freedom-journal-overview

8: Bullet Journaling

You were born to win, but to be a winner, you must plan to win, prepare to win, and expect to win.

—Zig Ziglar

Bullet journaling has taken the productivity and journaling world by storm, offering a quicker and more streamlined way of journaling and setting goals. There are hundreds of bullet-type journals on Amazon, replicating a concept that was the brainchild of a young emigrant from Vienna, Austria, who moved to the U.S. to attend college.

The idea for the official Bullet Journal and for the bullet journaling program was created by Ryder Carroll, a digital product designer and author. His personal struggles with learning disabilities as a child motivated and inspired him to develop his own strategies to be more focused and productive.

Through trial and error, he developed the bullet journaling methodology, one he says is "a mindfulness practice disguised as a productivity system."

He launched the first Bullet Journal in 2013 with the desire to help journal writers focus as much on the "why" of their actions as on their actual goals. He views goal-setting like any other mindfulness activity—as an intentional process.

Scientists[93] are suggesting that bullet journaling helps tackle a psychological phenomenon known as the Zeigarnik effect, which suggests we can better remember uncompleted tasks than completed ones. A bullet journal can clear your mind of those

---

93 https://www.inc.com/jessica-stillman/can-a-complicated-bullet-journal-help-you-get-more.html

nagging tasks and allow you to feel relief. Bullet journals also work as an extension of your memory, as our minds generally can deal with about three things at any given time.

Ryder Carroll's Bullet Journal runs around $25.00, but you can find similar journals on Amazon for $7.00 to $11.00. You can also replicate the bullet journaling concept in your own notebook.

With bullet journaling, the writer always journals by hand in a notebook—never with an app or by typing. Carroll recognizes the many benefits of writing in longhand but acknowledges that it can be time-consuming and unorganized.

Rather than asking journal writers to slog out complete sentences, he has developed what he calls *Rapid Logging* as the language of bullet journaling.

Rapid Logging is a way of capturing information in bullet lists using 60% less content than traditional writing. Entries are organized by topic and page numbers. The bullets of Rapid Logging are short-form sentences you pair with specific symbols that categorize your entries. These symbols include:

- • = Tasks

- – = Notes

- o = Events

Your bullet journal can serve as a planner, goal tracking tool, creative outlet, and traditional journal because there is so much flexibility in this style of journaling. You can tailor it to suit your journaling needs related to different parts of your life. This more graphical style of journaling invites doodling, using colored pens or pencils, highlighting, and other ways of expressing yourself artistically.

Advantages of Bullet Journaling

- Bullet journaling takes less time than traditional journaling because you are writing short sentences.

- Bullet journaling is structured in a way that keeps you organized at a glance.

- Bullet journaling lets you be more creative, intentional, and thoughtful about your goals and how you capture them on paper.

- Bullet journaling is adjustable and customizable.

Disadvantages of Bullet Journaling

- The bullet journaling symbols may be confusing or distracting for some journal writers.

- Bullet journaling doesn't work well for Morning Pages, stream of consciousness, or story form writing.

- Bullet journaling doesn't work for those who prefer typing over writing in longhand.

Who Is It For?

Bullet journaling might work well for ...

- Anyone who likes a more structured, organized, and streamlined method of journaling.

- Anyone who is more visual and prefers the use of symbols as shorthand for categories.

- Anyone with an artistic flair who likes to draw or doodle

along with journaling (although not essential for bullet journaling).

How to Get Started

1. Educate yourself on bullet journaling.

This concept is hard to explain through words alone, so we recommend that you spend an hour learning about the bullet journaling concept. Ryder Carroll has a detailed tutorial on his website,[94] including a 5-minute video walkthrough.

2. Choose your bullet journal.

You may want to use Carroll's Bullet Journal so that you are following the original intent of this journaling concept. But you can certainly use other bullet journals if you wish. Just be sure to do your research so you know what you are getting with a bullet journal and how the style compares to Carroll's concept. You can also use a blank journal to re-create the concept yourself. The "getting started" instructions below reflect Ryder Carroll's system for bullet journaling.

3. Add topic, date, and page numbers.

Before you begin writing any journal entry, get into the habit of adding a short, descriptive topic title at the top outer corner of the page. Also, number the page and add the date of your entry.

4. Begin writing using the Rapid Logging system.

The system will help organize your entries into three categories. Break down your logging system as follows:

Tasks are represented by a simple bullet point "•" and

---

94 https://bulletjournal.com/pages/learn

include any kind of actionable items. Each bullet has three additional states:

X = Task Complete

> = Task Migrated

< = Task Scheduled

Note: The bullet point is used for tasks because a bullet can easily be transformed into an X, or the < and > symbols with your pen. Just cover over the bullet with the new symbol based on the action you have taken.

Events are date-related entries represented by an "O" bullet.

- Events are scheduled events or events logged after they occur.
- Keep Event entries short and objective.

Notes are represented with a dash "–".

- Notes include facts, ideas, thoughts, and observations.
- Notes are entries that you want to remember but aren't immediately or necessarily actionable.
- Notes work well for meetings, lectures, or classroom notes.

Tasks, Events, and Notes don't have to be written in any particular order and can be mixed and matched within your journal entries. For example, you might have a list like this:

- *Pick up dry cleaning*

o *Dinner w/ Michael, 5:30*

> o Netflix premiere, 8:00
>
> – New band name: Outer Limits (?)

5. Nest your bullets as needed.

You may find that some tasks or notes fall under an event or that an event falls under a task or note. Feel free to nest your bullets accordingly. Here's an example:

> o Dinner w/ Michael, 5:30
>
> – Talk about band name
>
> – I pay this time
>
> • Plan end of month project
>
> o Meeting Thursday, 1:00
>
> – New spreadsheet format?

6. Use Signifiers for at-a-glance context.

Signifiers are additional symbols that help you quickly identify actions you need to take or the importance of particular actions. You can come up with your own Signifiers, but some examples might include:

> * = Priority action
>
> ! = Inspiration, great ideas, something you want to remember (it's often paired with a note)
>
> ◉ = Explore (an eye) for something that requires further research, information, or discovery

Note: If you create several Signifiers, be sure to create a Signifier Key in the front of your journal to help you remember them.

7. Build Modules (or Collections) to help collect and organize specific kinds of entries.

There are four core modules: The Index, Future Log, Monthly Log, and Daily Log.

- **The Index** should be in the front of your notebook to help you locate content in your Bullet Journal. You can add the topics of your Collections and their page numbers to the Index to quickly find and reference them.

- **The Future Log** is used to store items that either need to be scheduled months in advance or things that you want to get around to someday. It allows you to glimpse the brief outlines of the future goals you are working to achieve. You should review your Future Log each month to see if there's anything to put in your Monthly Log.

- **The Monthly Log** is a spread of two facing pages in your journal. On the left is a calendar page that gives you an overview of the month of schedule events or events that have happened. This is a quick view reference page. On the right is The Task Page, which is a bulleted list of your priorities and tasks for the month. To set up The Monthly Log, title the page with the current month's name. Then list all the dates of that month down the left margin, followed by the first letter of the corresponding day. Monday the 14th would be "14M." Leave some room in the left margin of the page to add Signifiers as needed.

- **The Daily Log** is for day-to-day use to Rapid Log your Tasks, Events, and Notes as they occur. Record the date at the top, but if you don't fill a page, add the next date wherever you left off and continue on. Don't set up your Daily Logs ahead of time because you never know how much space you'll need on a page.

8. Practice Monthly Migration.

You will start this in the second month of bullet journaling. Look at your previous entries for any unresolved tasks. "X" out your completed Tasks and assess whether the remaining open Tasks are still relevant. If a Task has become irrelevant, strike out the whole line, including the Bullet. If the Task still needs your attention, migrate it. Turn the "•" into ">" to signify that you've migrated that Task, then add it to the Task Page of your new Monthly Log.

Resources:

- The getting started section of the Bullet Journal website[95]
- Essentials Dot Matrix Notebook:[96] The journal that Steve always carries with him.
- Amanda Rach Lee:[97] Rachel has an entire YouTube channel dedicated to creating customized Bullet Journals.
- The Bullet Journal Method: Track the Past, Order the Present, Design the Future:[98] A new book written by Ryder Carroll.

---

95 http://bulletjournal.com/get-started/
96 https://www.amazon.com/gp/product/1441323716
97 https://www.youtube.com/user/amandarachlee
98 https://www.amazon.com/Bullet-Journal-Method-Present-Design-ebook/dp/B07B7C4F9C/

9: Make Your Own Journal

Unless you write yourself, you can't know how wonderful it is; I always used to bemoan the fact that I couldn't draw, but now I'm overjoyed that at least I can write. And if I don't have the talent to write books or newspaper articles, I can always write for myself.

—Anne Frank

You don't have to limit yourself to one type of journaling. Instead, you can create your own journal using an inexpensive lined notebook. You can pick and choose the different aspects of the various journaling techniques we've already outlined and create a unique set of prompts that work best for your needs.

You have two options with making your own journal: 1. You could combine a few simple prompts to focus on daily. 2. You can *deep dive* into one type of journaling technique and stick with it for a few days, weeks, or even months. So let's explore these options in more detail.

Option 1: Pick and choose different journaling prompts.

With this strategy, you want to pick a handful of simple prompts each day and write them down in a blank notebook. To help you get started, here are 20 journaling prompts and questions that will only require five minutes or less of your time:

1. Answer a gratitude question: "I am grateful for ___, because ___."

2. Finish with another simple gratitude question: "What am I looking forward to today (or tomorrow)?"

3. Use *New York Times* bestselling author (of *The Happiness*

Project) Gretchen Rubin's idea to write one or two sentences (max) about a significant thing that happened the previous day.

4. Write, "Today, I feel ..." and describe what you are experiencing mentally, physically, or emotionally at the moment you are writing.

5. Journal about the most interesting story, fact, or question you heard today and why it grabbed your attention.

6. Write about one of your favorite memories and go into detail about all aspects of the experience.

7. Journal about something you need to forgive yourself for and why you deserve forgiveness.

8. Think about something or someone you need to let go of and why it's time to let go.

9. Write a description of what your ideal day would look like.

10. What is one privilege you've taken for granted? How would your life be different without it?

11. Write out a list of ten things in your home you could easily get rid of without missing the items.

12. List ten positive qualities you love about your spouse, partner, best friend, or other significant person in your life.

13. Write about one consistent worry that appears in your life regularly and how you could address this worry.

14. Finish this sentence: "I could take better care of myself by _____."

15. Look out your window and describe everything you see in more detail than just writing, "a tree," "a bird," etc.

16. What is your inner voice trying to tell you? Journal about the answers that come up for you.

17. List the biggest distractions in your life that suck up time unnecessarily. Write about how you can manage or eliminate these distractions.

18. What is a negative pattern of behavior you catch yourself repeating? Write about an alternative way of behaving or reacting.

19. Write down ten ideas for simple acts of kindness you can offer during your days.

20. Journal about five ways you've grown as a person over the last five years.

Option 2: Deep dive into one type of journaling technique.

Another way you can create a unique journal is to write about a unique topic that will take more time but could be enlightening or entertaining. You can use the following ideas as part of your daily journal or as a separate journal that's dedicated to a specific practice. Here are a few ideas:

Write about Your Limiting Beliefs

At the core of our failures and inaction is a fear or belief that is holding us back. These beliefs create powerful emotions that are fed by repetitive negative thinking. The longer you've held onto a belief or fear, the more ingrained it is in your mind.

A journal is an excellent tool for exploring and healing from your limiting beliefs. Ask yourself why you have a certain belief and write down every reason you can think of. Then start undermining these reasons by listing evidence to the contrary. You might feel a certain way about yourself, but that doesn't make it true. There are hundreds of reasons why these limiting thoughts are not true or not completely true.

Write a Time Capsule Entry

Make your daily journal entry about something that is happening in the news. It could be the Olympics, the swearing in of a new president, or a medical breakthrough for cancer patients. Write down your thoughts about the event.

Describe how the country reacted during that period of time and include news clippings that will be of interest in the future. Wait ten or twenty years to read the entry again—you will be amazed at the details you included and the personal insight you recorded during that time.

Keep a Travel Journal

If you enjoy traveling, write about your experiences in different locations around the world. It's best to write in your journal as you are traveling so you can capture the precious details of your trips that could easily be forgotten. You can write about the food you eat, the excursions you experience, and even some of the people you meet.

If you haven't had the chance to travel much, write about places you would like to visit. When you are finally able to go, you can compare your experience with what you wrote.

Unless you travel every day, this isn't the best choice for building a daily journaling habit. But you can substitute a travel journal for your regular journal during the times you do travel.

Design a Character Sketch

We don't mean you should draw a portrait of yourself, though you can if you like. Instead, you can create a portrait in writing. Bring yourself or another individual to life by describing personality, appearance, moods, and style in a way that develops a character as an author might in a novel. You can even describe an imaginary individual if you prefer.

Journal about Your Personal History

Every day, write about something related to you, your family, and your life. Writing chronologically might help you trigger memories and think about friends and family members you haven't connected with in a while.

You might start with the story of your birth or background history on your parents and grandparents. Write about your childhood, your siblings, and your favorite memories.

Include entries on family traditions, vacations, and celebrations. Continue writing about your high school and college years, your young adult life, and your current life. Include photos, clippings, drawings, or anything that helps flesh out your personal history. This can become a great keepsake journal for your own family.

Write a Letter

This is a great way to talk to someone you don't get to see often. You can write to someone who has passed away, someone who lives far away from you, or even someone who lives in your home.

Maybe you have something to say to a person in your life, but you do not want to say it out loud. Writing a letter to them will help you organize your thoughts and sort through your feelings before you actually speak to them.

This is particularly helpful in your romantic relationships when you have a hard time communicating your feelings during conflict.

Write to an Imaginary Friend

Sometimes you need to tell others about your problems, but you might not be comfortable expressing yourself face-to-face. Writing in your journal to an imaginary (or real) friend is a great way to process your feelings with the thought that you are sharing them with a caring person, even if you never let anyone read what you've written. It allows you to "talk" to someone and organize your thoughts without being judged.

Write about Lessons Learned from a Book

If you have recently read a self-improvement or inspirational book, journal about what you learned from the book and how you plan to implement the lessons you learned. You can also write about the emotions the book evoked for you and how your mindset may have changed as a result of reading the book. Include some of your favorite quotes or passages from the book in your journal.

Try a Writing Sprint

Set your timer for five minutes and write until the time expires. It does not matter what you are writing about, simply make sure that your pencil is always moving. This is a great way to get your thoughts down on paper—and if your time is limited, it only requires five minutes. This is similar to Morning Pages writing, but it is for a limited time and does not require you to fill three full pages of writing.

Write One Sentence Each Day

Writing a lot can be discouraging for some, so if that sounds like you, start by writing one sentence a day in your daily journal. It will not take a lot of effort or time, but if the topic is something that interests you, you may even write more without realizing it. (Check out the *One Line a Day*[99] five-year journal if this interests you.)

Create Lists

When you draw a blank for new journaling ideas, just create a list of things you enjoy. This could be a list of movies, your favorite television shows, things you need to pack for your vacation, or even a grocery list. It's fun to go back through a list journal to see all of the things you've accomplished or that are meaningful to you.

Create a Mind Map

If you have been brainstorming for a big project, drawing out a mind map could help you get your ideas flowing. It will help you to see the bigger picture more clearly instead of focusing on a small part of the task at hand.

A mind map is a diagram that connects ideas and information around a central topic or problem. Mind-mapping also encourages linking or grouping concepts through natural associations that arise during the mapping process. This helps you come up with more ideas and find deeper meanings related to your topic.

Start with one idea in the center of your page and expand from

99 https://www.amazon.com/One-Line-Day-Five-Year-Memory/
dp/0811870197/ref=sr_1_3?ie=UTF8&qid=1537191750
&sr=8-3&keywords=one+line+a+day

that single thought. Write down anything that comes to mind. It may seem disorganized, but it will tell a story when the thought process is complete. While it may seem like you are adding extra steps to your journaling, it actually helps you decide what to write about.

Write a Letter to Your Younger Self

In this journaling exercise, you are writing to yourself at a younger age. It can be your childhood self or yourself just a few years back. You can offer advice, compassion, explanation, forgiveness, or praise.

Or you can simply recount an experience you had and how it impacted you as your adult self now. Try to see this younger self as a real and separate person when you write the letter.

Describe a Fictional Scenario

Picture yourself in a compelling story. You can use a prompt to paint an imaginary scenario and what unfolds.

Here are a few prompts you can use:

- You wake up on a beautiful Sunday morning, feeling happy and ready to take on the day. Then you remember. A wave of anxiety washes over you, and the beautiful day turns foreboding in an instant. Who are you? Where are you? What has happened to make you feel anxious and ruin your day?

- You're taking a walk on the beach early in the morning. The beach is nearly deserted. You notice something half buried in the sand, and when you examine it you see it's an old, rusted metal box. You open the box. What's inside the box? How does it make you feel? What are you going to do about it?

- You're sitting on the couch watching TV when you notice a receipt on your coffee table. You know you didn't leave a receipt there, and you live alone. What is the receipt for? How did it get on your coffee table?

Describe Your Surroundings

Simply write a paragraph or two about your surroundings. You can write in first person ("I am sitting at my desk, which is littered with papers and old coffee cups."), or write in third person, simply describing what you see ("The room is bleak and empty except for one old wooden chair.").

Challenge yourself to use descriptive language to set the scene. Rather than saying, "The light is shining through the window," you might say, "The morning sun is streaming through the window, spotlighting a million dancing dust particles and creating mottled shadows on my desk."

If you enjoy writing, this is an excellent form of journaling to improve your writing skills and vocabulary.

Be Creative

If you cannot figure out what to write in a daily journal, then you can simply make a creative entry of another type. Perhaps you like to draw. You can stencil a picture that you want to create, and you can even color it in if you wish.

If you do not have artistic talents, doodling is perfectly fine. Or use your journal to write down your favorite poems, quotes, or song lyrics. This is your journal, so use whatever creative means you wish to fill it.

These are just a few of hundreds of ideas for journaling. If you need more ideas, just Google "journal prompts" or visit Pinterest and type "journal writing ideas" in the search bar. You'll find more ideas for journaling than you have years to write!

Okay, now that you understand the nine journaling techniques, let's talk about how to turn one of these practices into a daily, "can't miss" habit. Up first, we'll review eight rules for keeping consistent with your journaling efforts.

8 Rules for Consistent Journaling

Journaling is like whispering to one's self and listening at the same time.

—Mina Murray

Rule 1: Be honest and candid with your thoughts.

This is important for working through your issues and personal challenges. If you have to censor what you're writing, you're limiting the effectiveness of journaling. Remember that this is your own private, personal journal. It is important in daily journaling that you be honest with yourself. If you can't do that, what's the point?

A journal is a reflection of your thoughts and emotions, so treat it that way. Don't limit what you write. Be open and honest about how you're feeling. If you can't be honest with yourself, you can't be honest with anyone. Would you censor thoughts in your head? Of course not! So why would you censor what you write in your journal?

This is one of the reasons it's good to avoid sharing your journal with anyone. When you know your journal is for your eyes only, you have the freedom to write whatever you want without worrying about anyone else's thoughts or judgments.

As you write, don't worry about your grammar or spelling—no matter how good or bad they are. If you can understand what you wrote in each entry, the grammar and spelling are fine.

One of the benefits of a handwritten journal entry is that you can make mistakes without having a red squiggly line show up beneath the word like it does in a word processor.

Rule 2: Set aside time daily.

One of the essential parts of starting a journaling habit isn't the writing itself but taking the time to do it. And doing it as if it's an important part of your day—every day.

We mean it—no excuses.

Start your daily journal off on the right foot by scheduling your writing for a set time every day. The time of day doesn't matter (except with Morning Pages), as long as it's a time that's convenient for you.

If you find your mind is most active in the morning, wake up 15 to 20 minutes earlier and jot down your thoughts then. This is also a great time to record your dreams from the previous night before you forget them. If you prefer to record everything after the day is over, then make journaling an evening activity you complete before you go to bed.

You get far more benefits from your journal when you write in it every day. Steve schedules his journal writing sessions in Todoist[100] on his phone so he always gets a reminder when it's time to write.

We all know that life happens from time to time, and you might miss a day. It's no big deal, but try to never miss more than two days. Once you do, it's easy to get into the routine of skipping your journaling, and then you have to rebuild the habit all over again.

---

100 https://todoist.com/

Rule 3: Create the right journaling environment.

We reviewed this rule in the beginning of the book, but it bears repeating. Journaling is about you and your thoughts. The best way to record those thoughts is to minimize distractions.

There's a reason that so many famous writers isolate themselves when they are writing their novels—because you need solitude to focus on your writing.

This doesn't mean you need to go to a cabin in the woods every time you want to journal, but you do need a quiet part of the room that's away from other people. Nowadays, it's also important to separate yourself from technology while journaling.

Here are a few suggestions to set up your environment:

- Turn off the TV
- Power down your computer
- Avoid your cell phone (or put it on silent mode)
- Find a quiet part of your home where family isn't around
- Get up early in the morning before anyone else

The key here is to make sure you won't be distracted if you hear a notification. This will make your journaling about you and your writing, and nothing else.

Rule 4: Protect your privacy.

Keeping your journal private is important, even if you don't care whether other people read it. You may not mind if someone reads your personal journal, but if you don't trust that your thoughts are private, you aren't going to be completely honest.

You may consciously or subconsciously avoid writing about

certain topics for fear of what others could think. This fear may hold you back from writing about stuff that matters.

Anytime you start a journal, you don't know with 100% certainty if someone will see it or not. You can take steps to protect your journal as much as possible, however.

The easiest way is to keep your journal with you at all times. This is also nice because you can jot down thoughts if something big occurs or if you have a sudden burst of inspiration.

You should also avoid letting anyone look at your journal—even just the cover. Tuck it away in your bag. Even people you trust will be more tempted when they see your journal, so keep it out of sight and out of mind.

Rule 5: Date each entry.

When it comes to your journal entries, if it's important enough to record, then it's important enough to date.

These are your private thoughts, but you will most likely look back on them later. Having a date above each entry can help you understand your thought process as it relates to important life events.

You can also see how you've progressed over time.

As mentioned earlier, memories fade with time. If you don't date your journal entries, you'll only have a general idea of when you wrote each entry.

Going one step further, let's say you decide to leave your journal behind for other people to read. If there aren't any dates, readers will have no idea when anything occurred.

Here's one final reason to date all your entries: It's easy and takes just seconds. All you have to do is write five or six numbers, depending on the month.

If you want to get creative with how you date your daily journal, you can include dated items such as receipts with certain entries.

Rule 6: Focus on simplicity.

One of Barrie's biggest problems when she started journaling was that she would spend too much time trying to find the perfect way to phrase what she wanted to write.

She wanted to say things "just the right way" to convey thoughts simply but elegantly—as she attempts to do on her blog and in her books.

But journaling is not professional writing.

When you try to journal perfectly formed thoughts, you don't get nearly as many thoughts down on paper. Your journaling takes longer, and then journaling begins to feel like a chore instead of a cathartic activity. Even if you try to be erudite and artful with your journaling, you still won't be completely satisfied with your writing. That's human nature.

Perfection is unattainable, and chasing it is an exercise in futility. Just get your honest thoughts down on paper as they come to you. Remember that you're not writing a college term paper or a novel. Quality and depth of your writing isn't important in journaling.

Rule 7: Write by hand if possible.

Steve has always preferred typing, due to his horrific handwriting. If someone with handwriting as bad as his recommends that you write your journal entries by hand, it's a sign that it must be pretty important.

Steve can easily type 50 to 60 words per minute, and you would think that makes it smarter to type journal entries. After all, more words equal more thoughts that you can capture. However, the slowness of writing by hand is better for developing and connecting with your thoughts as you write them, as we outlined earlier.

That said, if you are a dyed-in-the-wool typist and won't journal unless you hear the pitter-patter of fingers on keys (or thumbs on a phone), then by all means, type away. The important thing is that you journal—in longhand or with a digital device.

Rule 8: It's okay to quit.

Overall, we recommend doing SOME type of journaling. But you might find you're not enjoying the process of journaling. If this is you, we recommend that you try something else. It took Steve a few tries before he finally focused on a combination of goal journaling through Evernote one time a week and idea journaling throughout his week whenever he needs to work through a problem.

You may go months without feeling the desire to journal, and if so, give yourself permission to take a break. If it starts to feel more like a chore than a joy, it's not serving you. The good news is that you can return to journaling whenever you wish. There's no expiration date!

One of the best ways to revive your desire to journal is to go back and read previous journals. You may be inspired to pick up where you left off or try a new form of journaling that you haven't attempted before. We've outlined plenty of options for you!

All right, we're now in the homestretch. In the next (and final) chapter, we will cover how to create the journaling habit so it becomes an important part of your day.

How to Make the Journaling Habit Stick

Habit is a cable; we weave a thread each day,
and at last we cannot break it.

—Horace Mann

Building a new habit can be hard. Your brain doesn't make it easy for you. As much as you want to create a new habit and sustain it, your desire to keep at it begins to fade after a few days or weeks. At first, it's fun, then it's challenging, then it's work, and finally, it's forgotten.

Why does this happen?

It has nothing to do with your willpower or energy. It has to do with brain chemistry. You haven't given your brain enough time to fully rewire itself to incorporate your habit as part of your daily routine. And that's what has to happen—you have to retrain your brain.

Most of us jump into a new habit full force. For example, if we decide we need to lose weight, we immediately change our diet, start exercising, write down everything we eat, and begin weighing ourselves.

But each one of these changes comprises a series of many smaller habits. By deciding to lose weight, you are asking your brain to accommodate ten or more new habits rather than just one. Your brain can't handle that. It's like asking a toddler to pass advanced chemistry. No wonder we give up.

But science has taught us that there is a way to develop a new habit that minimizes the chance you'll throw in the towel. Here's what you need to do to make journaling an automatic, daily behavior—just like brushing your teeth, putting on clothes, and brewing your morning coffee.

1. Pick a journaling technique. (And stick to it!)

As you've seen—we have profiled nine different ways to journal. The problem? It's easy to feel *overwhelmed* by all the options. In fact, one of the main reasons people stop journaling is they don't enjoy the experience. And in our opinion, people often quit because they didn't pick the right journaling technique for them.

So that's why the first step of the habit-building process is to review the nine techniques that we've profiled and pick one that best resonates with you.

Simply go back through the nine journaling techniques and review each of the "Who Is It For?" sections. Ask yourself: Does this strategy sound like a habit I'd enjoy doing every day?

Furthermore, ask yourself a few questions like:

- Do I have a goals-oriented personality? (Then *Goal Journaling* might make a good choice.)
- Am I an entrepreneur or a creative personality? (Then *Idea Journaling* can help you generate a wealth of inspirational thoughts.)
- Do I have a limited amount of time each morning? (Then *Morning Pages* might not be the best option for you.)

- Do I frequently find myself anxious, fearful, or generally unhappy with the world around me? (Then *Gratitude* or *Mindfulness Journaling* can help.)

- Do I need an all-in-one solution for journaling and managing my day? (Then *Bullet Journaling* can become your secret weapon.)

Overall, we don't believe there is one "right" journaling technique. Everyone has their own unique tastes and personal preferences. So your job with this first step is to identify the option that works best for your personal situation.

2. Start *really* small.

Most people want to create big change as quickly as possible.

They want to go from zero to four gym sessions every week, switch to a healthy diet overnight, and meditate for 20 minutes every day even though they've barely managed five minutes in the past. Biting off more than you can chew sets you up for failure.

Begin your new habit in small time bites. **If journaling is new for you, focus on doing it for five minutes or less per day.** Do this for a week or so, and gradually add time over the successive weeks until you reach your desired journaling time.

Always focus on establishing the actual *habit behavior* first and making it part of your day. Never increase the effort before it has become a natural part of what you do every day.

3. Identify a trigger or cue.

Science has confirmed the best way to ensure you perform a new habit is by having a trigger that cues you to perform it.

You mentally attach your new habit to this cue, and you have a built-in reminder system to get it done.

There are several different types of triggers you can use to do the job.

Trigger #1: Time

You can use a specific time of day as a reminder to perform your habit. For example, waking up in the morning or getting into bed at night could be your trigger to write in your journal. Or maybe you want to write just before or after your lunch hour.

If you choose a random time, like 3:00 in the afternoon, you'll need to set an alarm on your phone or watch to remind you.

Trigger #2: Location

Research studies[101] by David Neal and Wendy Wood from Duke University have revealed that new habits are easier to perform in new locations. The theory is that since we already assign existing habits to specific locations, it's harder to consistently perform new habits in these locations because we're triggered to perform the old one.

A new location gives you a blank slate that isn't associated with previous triggers for existing habits. We suggest that you pick a specific location for your journal writing efforts. This could be a quiet room in your house that's rarely used. Or if space is an issue, you could journal while sitting in your favorite chair. It doesn't matter what you pick. What's important is to stay consistent with this location.

---

101 http://journals.sagepub.com/doi/abs/10.1111/j.1467-8721.2006.00435.x

Trigger #3: Previous Habits

You can use an established habit as the trigger for your new habit. For example, you decided to journal immediately after you make your morning coffee or after you wash your face before bed.

This is part of the process of "habit stacking" that Steve covers in his book by the same name (*Habit Stacking: 127 Small Changes to Improve Your Health, Wealth, and Happiness*[102]).

Just be sure you choose a habit trigger that you perform every day at about the same time. For a new habit to become automatic, you need to practice it every day in the beginning. A variable trigger that isn't daily will not help you remember to perform your habit.

4. Get hooked on your habit.

Have you ever noticed how hard it is to let go of a project when you've invested a lot of effort into it? We can use this tendency to our advantage by using what comedian Jerry Seinfeld calls the "Don't break the chain" strategy.

Seinfeld used this method to become a better comic by writing a new joke every day. Each time he completed his daily writing, he put a big red X for the day on his calendar. Within a few days, he had a chain he didn't want to break.

This is a clever strategy you can use to create a visual reminder of how much effort you've invested in your journaling practice.

---

102 https://www.amazon.com/Habit-Stacking-Changes-Improve-Happiness-ebook/dp/B06XP2B5QC/ref=sr_1_2?ie=UTF8&qid=1537208647&sr=8-2&keywords=habit+stacking

You'll likely find that the longer the chain grows, the harder you'll fight to keep it going.

So, get a calendar, put a marker next to it, and get to work journaling. Your only job next is to never break the chain.

Or if you prefer a digital way to track your efforts, you could use one of the four apps we mentioned in the section on journaling tools:

- StridesApp.com[103]
- Coach.me[104]
- HabitHub[105]
- Todoist[106]

Just as we discussed when picking a trigger, it doesn't matter what device you use to track this habit. What's important is to pick one and stick with it!

5. Celebrate your small wins.

If you're like most people, you're much better at beating yourself up for a bad performance than you are at rewarding yourself for a good one.

When it comes to managing ourselves, for some reason, we seem to prefer the stick to the carrot. And that's a shame because research has shown that celebrating your progress is crucial to maintaining motivation.

---

103 https://www.stridesapp.com/
104 https://www.coach.me/
105 http://www.thehabithub.com/
106 http://todoist.com

Each time you reward yourself for making progress, no matter how small, you activate the reward circuitry in your brain.

That releases some key chemicals, which make you experience feelings of achievement and pride. These emotions, in turn, empower you to take action and create bigger successes in the future.

So, reward yourself for each step in the right direction, no matter how small they happen to be. Every time you put an X on your calendar showing you wrote in your journal, do something that makes you happy.

Need some ideas? Consider these:

- Eat a piece of chocolate.
- Go outside and savor the fresh air.
- Call your best friend.
- Surf the net for a few minutes.
- Listen to your favorite song.
- Make a cup of tea and sip it slowly.
- Read a few pages of your book.
- Get a long hug from your spouse or partner.
- Close your eyes and rest for a few minutes.

There are countless ways to reward yourself for sticking to the journaling habit. If you'd like to learn more, check out Steve's blog post with 155 ideas on the subject.[107]

---

107 https://www.developgoodhabits.com/reward-yourself/

6. Surround yourself with supporters.

The people around you have a surprisingly big impact on your behavior. One study[108] showed that if you have a friend who becomes obese, your risk of obesity increases by 57%—even if your friend lives hundreds of miles away!

Other research has shown that we tend to feel the same way and adopt the same goals as the people we spend the most time with. So, one way to dramatically increase your chances of success with journaling is to make sure you have the right people in your corner.

Be sure you have the support and encouragement of your spouse, partner, friends, and anyone who might know that you are committed to the journaling habit. Let them know that you're working to develop this habit, ask them to encourage you, and acknowledge your success with it.

7. Set up accountability.

Many of us don't tell others when we begin a new habit because we don't want to be embarrassed if we fail. But public accountability can be a great motivator.

Accountability can be powered by integrity, fear of embarrassment, pride, or shame. Whatever the reason for using it, accountability works. It provides the element of tension to get the job done—to make something happen that might not have happened without it.

Announce your new journaling habit on Facebook or other social media platform, or email all of your friends to let them know.

---

108 https://www.nytimes.com/2007/07/25/health/25iht-fat.4.6830240.html

Then create a daily system of reporting your progress to these people.

Be sure you tell your accountability partner or group exactly how you want them to hold you accountable. Do you want to be called out if you haven't followed through? Or do you want only positive reinforcement when you get the job done? This is particularly important with your spouse or partner and family members, as you don't want accountability to feel like shaming or nagging.

Well, that's it for building the journaling habit. Really, it comes down to starting small, focusing on consistency, rewarding yourself for those small wins, and not quitting whenever you encounter an obstacle.

Final Thoughts on *Effortless Journaling*

Keep a notebook. Travel with it, eat with it, sleep with it.
Slap into it every stray thought that flutters up in your brain.
Cheap paper is less perishable than gray matter, and lead pencil
markings endure longer than memory.

—Jack London

Well, we've reached the end of *Effortless Journaling*. You now know how to:

1. Identify the perfect journaling technique based on your background and personal preferences;

2. Find the time to journal—even if you have a hectic schedule;

3. Know *what* to journal about and how to find inspiration in the world around you;

4. Pick the best journaling tools to get started with this habit;

5. Write without fear or self-censorship because the topics resonate with your internal thoughts;

6. Combine journaling with mindfulness so you're always living in the present moment;

7. Turn journaling into a permanent "can't miss" habit.

Journaling can become your secret weapon to living a fulfilled life. In fact, this habit can become the foundation upon which you build other powerful routines into your daily life.

There's something magical about putting your thoughts down on paper every day and analyzing all your experiences. You get to the heart of what you *really* think. You learn to appreciate what you have in life. And you can create an action plan for what you want to accomplish in the next few weeks, months, or even years.

Simply put: Journaling can transform your life—*if* you're willing to commit to building this habit.

Now it's up to you.

We encourage you to *not* just close out this book. Instead, grab a low-cost notebook and pen, then go quickly review this material *one more time*. Get started by identifying the one journaling technique that resonates with your life right now. Commit to it for the next 30 days. After that, review the eight rules on staying consistent with the habit. Next, implement the action steps for making the journaling habit stick. Finally, be sure to schedule five to ten minutes a day so you can start journaling.

Sounds like a plan, right?

Well, we hope you found this book to be helpful. We wish you the best of luck and hope that you discover the value of setting aside time each day to journal.

Cheers,

S.J. Scott & Barrie Davenport

One Last Reminder ...

We've covered a wealth of information in this book, but that doesn't mean your journaling education ends here. In fact, we are offering a free digital product that's <u>exclusive</u> to readers of *Effortless Journaling*.

If you'd like to get started right away, you can grab a PDF version of our bestselling physical journal:

The 90-Day Gratitude Journal: A Mindful Practice for a Lifetime of Happiness

Simple follow this link to grab your free PDF today:

https://www.developgoodhabits.com/90day-gratitude

Thank You!

Before you go, we'd like to say thank you for purchasing our book.

You could have picked from dozens of books on habit development, but you took a chance and checked out this one.

So, big thanks for purchasing this book and reading all the way to the end.

Now we'd like to ask for a small favor. Could you please take a minute or two and leave a review for this book on Amazon?

This feedback will help us continue to write the kind of books that help you get results. And if you loved it, please let us know. ☺

More Books by Steve

How to Stop Procrastinating: A Simple Guide to Mastering Difficult Tasks and Breaking the Procrastination Habit

10-Minute Mindfulness: 71 Habits for Living in the Present Moment

Habit Stacking: 127 Small Actions to Improve Your Health, Wealth, and Happiness

Novice to Expert: 6 Steps to Learn Anything, Increase Your Knowledge, and Master New Skills

Declutter Your Mind: How to Stop Worrying, Relieve Anxiety, and Eliminate Negative Thinking

The Miracle Morning for Writers: How to Build a Writing Ritual That Increases Your Impact and Your Income

10-Minute Digital Declutter: The Simple Habit to Eliminate Technology Overload

10-Minute Declutter: The Stress-Free Habit for Simplifying Your Home

The Accountability Manifesto: How Accountability Helps You Stick to Goals

Confident You: An Introvert's Guide to Success in Life and Business

Exercise Every Day: 32 Tactics for Building the Exercise Habit (Even If You Hate Working Out)

The Daily Entrepreneur: 33 Success Habits for Small Business Owners, Freelancers and Aspiring 9-to-5 Escape Artists

Master Evernote: The Unofficial Guide to Organizing Your Life with Evernote (Plus 75 Ideas for Getting Started)

Bad Habits No More: 25 Steps to Break Any Bad Habit

Habit Stacking: 97 Small Life Changes That Take Five Minutes or Less

To-Do List Makeover: A Simple Guide to Getting the Important Things Done

23 Anti-Procrastination Habits: How to Stop Being Lazy and Overcome Your Procrastination

S.M.A.R.T. Goals Made Simple: 10 Steps to Master Your Personal and Career Goals

115 Productivity Apps to Maximize Your Time: Apps for iPhone, iPad, Android, Kindle Fire and PC/iOS Desktop Computers

Writing Habit Mastery: How to Write 2,000 Words a Day and Forever Cure Writer's Block

Daily Inbox Zero: 9 Proven Steps to Eliminate Email Overload

Wake Up Successful: How to Increase Your Energy and Achieve Any Goal with a Morning Routine

10,000 Steps Blueprint: The Daily Walking Habit for Healthy Weight Loss and Lifelong Fitness

70 Healthy Habits: How to Eat Better, Feel Great, Get More Energy and Live a Healthy Lifestyle

Resolutions That Stick! How 12 Habits Can Transform Your New Year

More Books by Barrie

Declutter Your Mind: How to Stop Worrying, Relieve Anxiety, and Eliminate Negative Thinking

10-Minute Digital Declutter: The Simple Habit to Eliminate Technology Overload

10-Minute Declutter: The Stress-Free Habit for Simplifying Your Home

201 Relationship Questions: The Couple's Guide to Building Trust and Emotional Intimacy

Self-Discovery Questions: 155 Breakthrough Questions to Accelerate Massive Action

Sticky Habits: 6 Simple Steps to Create Good Habits That Stick

Finely Tuned: How To Thrive As A Highly Sensitive Person or Empath

Peace of Mindfulness: Everyday Rituals to Conquer Anxiety and Claim Unlimited Inner Peace

Confidence Hacks: 99 Small Actions to Massively Boost Your Confidence

Building Confidence: Get Motivated, Overcome Social Fear, Be Assertive, and Empower Your Life for Success

The 52-Week Life Passion Project: Uncover Your Life Passion

Made in the USA
San Bernardino, CA
23 November 2018